To
Howard
12-25-86
One Nancy
and
Tommy

THE CIVIL WAR

THE CIVIL WAR

DOUGLAS WELSH

Galahad Books · New York City

A Bison Book

First Published in the US by
Galahad Books
a division of A & W Publishers, Inc.
95 Madison Avenue
New York
New York 10016

Copyright © 1982 Bison Books Limited

Produced by
Bison Books Limited
4 Cromwell Place
London SW7

Library of Congress Catalog Card Number
81-86550

ISBN 0-88365-600-0

Printed in Hong Kong

CONTENTS

1 A NATION DIVIDED

The Civil War is unique among American wars, with the devastating characteristics of all civil wars, in which nations are divided within themselves and their people take up arms against each other. In retrospect however its great battles, personalities, and the transition in the art of warfare produced an aura of romanticism which is found in no other American war. It was a costly war which left a lingering bitterness but no traitors are remembered and the United States reveres men of both the North and South as national heroes.

Both simple and complex causes resulted in the American Civil War. Two nations had risen from one country. The North had developed into a vast industrial region and was the primary center of immigration and population. 'New blood' and industrialization kept the North in pace with the rest of the industrialized world. Progress was the primary goal. In the South time appeared to stand still. It remained an agricultural center with manufacturing industries in a small number of major cities. Population growth had been slow by comparison with the North and the economic and social structures continued to be based on a slave system and 'King Cotton.'

These were the simple differences. The complex issues followed the same fundamental lines. The political structure of the United States had been maintained and kept relatively in balance between North and South, by the addition of states to the Union in such a way that neither sector took a dominant role in the governing processes of the country. As time passed the Southern ideology and its peculiar institution, slavery, began to suffer. More states joined the Union with political and economic views closely aligned to and dependent on the traditions of the North. The difference in population between North and South caused a shift in the balance of power within the House of Representatives as more Northern Representatives were added to the rolls. The Southern States became almost entirely dependent on the United States Senate to maintain and uphold its way of life. So long as the Senate remained balanced the tensions felt by the Southern states could be eased. However in the years just prior to the war that balance of power deteriorated as it had done in the House. Taxes and tariffs were imposed which handi-capped the South's trade and economy. Abolitionists were making strong protests in an effort to put an end to slavery. Consequently the Southern states felt threatened by the Federal Government. They claimed that the government of the United States of America was no longer fairly representing the South. Legislation was being forced upon them and the Southern people found the situation increasingly intolerable.

From these issues arose the fundamental cause of the American Civil War – States' Rights. Southern political leaders realized that since the Federal Government no longer appeared to represent their ideologies, interests and life styles, their sovereign states' rights were being eroded and would soon be lost. The principle was set forth that, as the nation had been originally formed by the voluntary union of states for the common good, a state could voluntarily withdraw from a union which threatened the perceived good of that particular state. It was also proposed that a group of states which felt similarly inclined could form a new union which served their needs and purposes.

Northern leaders found the idea preposterous. The concept that the people owed allegiance to their individual states before their national government was unthinkable. If such a line of thought was allowed to persist, laws and decisions made by the Federal Government could be ignored at the whim of the individual states. In such a case there could be no national government and the United States would collapse. The future of the United States of America depended on which ideology would prevail.

Twenty-two states, including the newly formed state of West Virginia, rallied to the Northern cause. These states had a total population of 22,000,000. Ninety-two percent of the industrial capacity of the United States lay in the Northern states, as well as most of the raw materials such as coal and iron ore. Agricultural support was found in the western states. Transportation by railroad, river and road gave the North a clear advantage in the rapid movement of goods and materials. The North also maintained an advantage at sea. The merchant fleets of the North could continue to trade with foreign markets, compensating for any deficiencies which might arise as a result of war. Another advantage which would become evident only after the war began was the fact that most of the regular army troops would remain loyal to the Union. In short, the Union held a definite superiority in manpower, natural resources, agricultural potential, transportation and financial stability.

By contrast the 11 Southern states which would officially create the Confederate States of America had a population of approximately 9,000,000, 3,500,000 of whom were blacks. However as slaves represented the bulk of the labor force, a higher percentage of white males would be available for military duty than in the North. Also the male population was for the most part more accustomed to firearms and more skilled in the art of horsemanship than in the North. One of the primary advantages of the Confederate States, particularly in the early war

years, was its officer corps. The cream of the officer corps of the United States Army were Southerners, who rallied to the call of their individual states. The Union military command had hoped to persuade Robert E Lee to take command of all Union forces, but he, like so many of his contemporaries, decided to serve the Confederacy. General Winfield Scott, Chief of Staff of the Federal Army likened the loss of Lee to the loss of 50,000 veteran troops on a battlefield. The Union Army was crippled by the defection of its best officers to the Southern cause. Finally Southerners realized that if war began it would be the problem of the North to conquer the South. The Confederate armies would be defending their ideals and their homeland, which the Southern leaders believed gave them the most powerful advantage.

Left: slavery was only one of the issues which divided North and South before the outbreak of the Civil War in 1861. Below: Union seapower gave the North the means to isolate the Confederacy by blockading her coastlines.

7

The South would fight to achieve States' Rights while the North would strive to preserve the integrity of the Union. Given their individual strengths and weaknesses each had to devise and develop its own particular strategy. A defensive war was the most logical option for the South. The North was quite obviously divided in its feelings about the war and a great effort would be made to force the North to abandon hostilities as its population wearied of a prolonged conflict. Confederate plans to seize Washington and invade West Virginia and Pennsylvania were formulated early in the war. However the primary goal of the Confederate leaders was to turn the Northern populace against the war as quickly as possible before the might of the North's industry and manpower could be brought to bear.

The North had three main goals. One was to cripple the nonindustrial economy of the South by blockading the coastlines of the Confederate States. Another was to divide the Confederacy by capturing the Mississippi River and to isolate regions of the South by eliminating the few interior railroads. The most important, ever-present goal was the capture of the Confederate capital, which after May 1861 was Richmond, Virginia. The capture of their opponent's capital was equally dominant in both the North and South as the fall of the capital was synonymous with defeat.

On 30 December 1860 South Carolina seceded

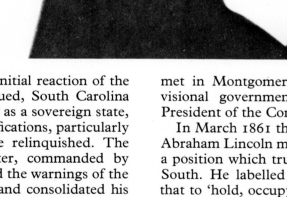

Right: Abraham Lincoln's election as President in 1861 brought the issue of secession to a head and precipitated the outbreak of the Civil War.

from the Union. Although the initial reaction of the Federal Government was subdued, South Carolina moved swiftly to claim its rights as a sovereign state, demanding that all Federal fortifications, particularly those in Charleston harbor, be relinquished. The harbor garrison in Fort Sumter, commanded by Major Robert Anderson, ignored the warnings of the government of South Carolina and consolidated his 70-man force to prepare for any action which might be taken against him. The authorities in South Carolina were furious at the refusal of the Federal Government to relinquish its fortifications and throughout January and February 1861 other Southern States showed their sentiments by joining South Carolina in seceding from the Union. Representatives from those states

met in Montgomery, Alabama, to organize a provisional government, electing Jefferson Davis as President of the Confederate States of America.

In March 1861 the newly elected Union President Abraham Lincoln made his inaugural address, stating a position which truly satisfied neither the North or South. He labelled secession unlawful and warned that to 'hold, occupy or possess' any property of the Federal Government in any of those seceded states was inherently wrong. However he also acknowledged the fact that he did not want war and that military action at that particular time would make him appear as an aggressor in the delicate situation. Three days later the Confederate Congress called for the enlistment of 100,000 men to protect their new nation.

2 THE ROAD TO SHILOH

When Major Anderson consolidated his forces in Fort Sumter he had no intention of committing an act of war. Given the mood of the Southern community in Charleston, Anderson was merely taking precautionary measures. However those measures evoked an angry, aggressive response and demands that Brigadier General PGT Beauregard make preparations to attack the fort if necessary. The Confederate Government expected Fort Sumter to surrender peacefully, but Beauregard's repeated requests for surrender were refused. Anderson realized that resistance against the Confederate batteries that ringed the harbor was futile, but as commander of the garrison he could not relinquish the fortification without orders from a higher authority. Finally Beauregard gave Anderson formal warning that unless the garrison surrendered Fort Sumter would be taken by force. Anderson replied that he respected Beauregard's position, but he must deny the request.

At 0400 hours 12 April 1861, the bombardment of Fort Sumter began. The isolated, undermanned garrison could not possibly respond to the Confederate batteries with any substantial retaliation and Anderson gave strict orders that all efforts were to be made to cause the least possible damage to Charleston. For the most part the garrison forces simply remained in their fortified bunkers during the bombardment. By Sunday afternoon, 14 April, with part of the fort ablaze, Anderson surrendered the garrison. A 50-gun salute was fired as the Stars and Stripes was lowered. During the salute the garrison force sustained its only fatality, in an accidental powder explosion. Anderson was then permitted to march his troops with full military honors aboard waiting Union vessels bound for Northern ports. Although Fort Sumter was the first battle of the Civil War, it was actually little more than a skirmish. The sole importance of the incident lay in the fact that a state of war now existed between the Union and the Confederacy.

The opening days of the war created confusion in both the North and South. Although both governments called for large numbers of volunteers, the majority of recruits had little or no military training. Adequate training programs were essential if they were to be of any use to their respective governments. Raw recruits had to be converted into soldiers and the

Above: a Union recruiting poster appeals for volunteers.

army which could best accomplish that transition before the first major confrontation might win not only the battle but the war. It was a naive view, but one which was shared by the majority of leaders and the civilian population as well.

When Virginia seceded the vulnerability and isolation of Washington, the Union capital, became painfully evident. As Richmond was so near to Washington, it was obvious that a major part of the war effort would be concentrated in that region, as each side attempted to capture the opposing capital, but the war would not be confined to the East. Union armies were forming in Ohio and Illinois and along the Mississippi River. Confederate forces quickly arose to oppose the Union forces and the first battles of the war were fought in Missouri and West Virginia, with the Union winning quick though minor victories.

By July 1861 preparations were being completed for the first campaign of the war. Manassas Junction on the Bull Run Creek was the site of that first major confrontation, the battle which many believed would decide the fate of the Union or Confederacy. The Union army around Washington had reached 50,000 men and was commanded by Brigadier General Irwin McDowell. The Confederate forces located around

Manassas numbered approximately 20,000 troops with an additional 11,000 men at Winchester, Virginia, and 3000 men at Acquia Creek. The main Confederate forces at Manassas were commanded by the reigning Confederate hero General Beauregard, but General Joseph E Johnston at Winchester was the ranking Confederate officer in the region.

The Union plan of attack against Manassas was simple. McDowell was to leave 15,000 troops to protect Washington and march his 35,000-man army to Manassas. There he would engage and defeat Beauregard and then march on to attack and capture Richmond. The problem was that, while Union politicians and newspapers demanded that McDowell do something with his large army before their three-month enlistment expired, the troops were not sufficiently trained or disciplined to accomplish their goal. Once the march to Manassas began, McDowell realized that it was virtually impossible to maneuver his army and it took him two-and-a-half days to cover only 20 miles.

The Confederates had their own problems, primarily the concentration of the available forces in the Manassas area. Johnston was faced with the task of maneuvering his Winchester forces to rendezvous with Beauregard before McDowell could reach Manassas, without alerting Major General Robert Patterson and his Union army of 18,000 men at Martinsburg, Virginia. Through the deployment of a superb cavalry screen, commanded by Colonel JEB Stuart, Johnston was able to slip away from Winchester with 9000 men. It was two days later when Patterson realized the ruse, which permitted Johnston to join Beauregard and effectively eliminated Patterson's forces from the impending battle.

On 18 July McDowell sent a small contingent forward to assess the Confederate strength. Brigadier General James Longstreet's brigade drove the Union force back in chaos. McDowell's reaction to the initial

Confederate success was to waste two days reconnoitering the area, reorganizing his troops and moving supplies from his rear area. Those two days gave Johnston the time he needed to reach Manassas. By the morning of 21 July McDowell and Johnston with their respective armies were on the battlefield and prepared to launch their attacks. The battle plan for each army was an assault on the left flank of its opponent. However misunderstandings and mismanagement by the Confederate command in their attempts to initiate the attack caused Johnston to abandon his own maneuvers in the face of the Union threat.

The Union attack was divided into two main thrusts. The main assault was commanded by McDowell and was to cross Bull Run Creek near Sudley Church wide of the Confederate left flank. The Union First Division was to cross the Stone Bridge before dawn, as a diversionary tactic to hold the focus of attention until McDowell could launch his flank attack. At 0515 hours Union forces began their assault at the Stone Bridge, but it was soon obvious that they were making no great effort to advance against the weaker Confederate forces defending the area. The attack on the left flank, planned for 0700 hours, did not materialize until 0900 hours and the restraint of the Union forces at the Stone Bridge had not caused any major shift in the Confederate defenses elsewhere on the battlefield.

The Union main attack was swiftly spotted and Colonel Nathan Evans rapidly maneuvered the bulk of his forces to a defensive position near the Warrenton Turnpike. Brigades of Colonel AE Burnside's Second Division were the first to encounter the Confederate defenders. They were later joined by other brigades of that division and elements of the Union Third Division, but the Confederate defenders held fast. The piecemeal character of the Union attack allowed the outnumbered Confederates to blunt the frontal assault. However Brigadier General William Tecum-

Left and above right: the First Battle of Manassas, also known as Bull Run, was the first major engagement of the war.

seh Sherman's Union brigade arrived from across Bull Run Creek, catching the Confederates on their right flank and breaking their defense.

The Confederate troops fled across the Warrenton Turnpike to the slopes of Robinson House and Henry House Hills. Cresting the hill, General Barnard Bee espied the well-trained Harper's Ferry forces of General Thomas Jonathan Jackson standing in line formation beyond the crest of Henry House Hill. In his efforts to rally his forces, Bee exclaimed, 'Look! There is Jackson standing like a stone wall. Rally behind the Virginians!' Bee's description of the Confederate line would make the nickname 'Stonewall' Jackson one of the most familiar of the American Civil War. The battle raged at Henry House Hill as Jackson's troops held their ground. At one point an error in judgment exposed the Union artillery, which was attacked and captured by Jeb Stuart's cavalry and elements of Jackson's force. The numerically superior

Union forces were able to withstand the addition of Brigadier General E Kirby Smith's forces to the Confederate defense, but it was obvious that both sides were tiring and that whichever force was the first to receive reinforcements would be victorious. In the distance reinforcements appeared, but it was impossible to distinguish to which army they belonged. Finally a breeze displayed Confederate colors and announced the arrival of Colonel Jubal Early's brigade. The Confederate lines surged forward and the Union lines dissolved.

The battle technically ended with the events at Henry House Hill. Initially the Union forces retreated in good order toward Washington. However the explosion of Confederate artillery shells on the road which led to the Union capital panicked the politicians and socialites who had come out from the city to view the battle. Their panic spread to the Union troops and a rout began which continued until

Above: Captain Nathan Lyon led Union support in Missouri.

Above: General Winfield Scott commanded the Union Army.

all were safely within the city. The actual number of troops committed to the First Battle of Manassas was approximately 18,000 for both the Union and Confederacy, but there were approximately 900 more Union troops killed, wounded or missing. The Confederates could claim a major victory. Not only had they retained the battlefield, they had also captured satisfactory quantities of arms, ammunition, equipment and supplies. Perhaps most importantly, the first battle of the Civil War illustrated the need for consistency in uniforms and flags. A great deal of confusion and deterioration of morale was caused by the fact that it was not easy to distinguish between friend and foe. Initially 'cadet gray' uniforms were most widely used, supplemented by articles of civilian dress, but elaborate, impractical uniforms such as the French Zouave dress were also worn. The Union opted for a dark blue jacket with trousers of various shades of blue. The Confederacy chose a gray jacket with trousers of gray or light blue, as those materials were widely accessible. The flag of the Confederate States of America was revised, from one which closely resembled the Stars and Stripes to the more distinct Stars and Bars, with 13 stars representing the 11 seceded states as well as Missouri and Kentucky.

With the defeat at Manassas, President Lincoln decided that the Union forces required new leadership and Major General George B McClellan was called upon to replace McDowell as commander of the Union army at Washington. Shortly thereafter General Winfield Scott retired and McClellan was given the added responsibility of commander of all Union armies. McClellan's victories in West Virginia, particularly at Rich Mountain, in the early months of the war, earned him the self-proclaimed title 'New Napoleon.' Whether he in fact deserved that title is questionable. Although McClellan was an excellent

administrator with a flair for organization, it became evident as the months passed that he seemed disinclined to put his army to the test in battle. Union troops and the newspapers began to question his abilities and in the South he became a source of sarcastic amusement.

There was a lull in activity in the East after Manassas and attention was primarily focussed on the Western Region. In Missouri the newly promoted Brigadier General Nathaniel Lyon was experiencing a series of successes and appeared to be leading the Union to victory in that state. In the early fall that momentum was lost, when Lyon was killed on 10 August at the Battle of Wilson's Creek. Kentucky, which was struggling to remain neutral in spite of the South's claims that it belonged to the Confederacy, was being divided from within and without. In September Confederate commander Major General Leonidas Polk seized Columbus, Kentucky. Shortly thereafter Brigadier General Ulysses S Grant seized Paduca and the lines were finally drawn. The governor of Kentucky declared for the Union, while the vast majority of legislators rallied to the Confederate cause. The rift resulted in armies of both factions entering in the hope of achieving quick victories, which would assure the allegiance of the state to their respective causes. However no engagement of significant influence occurred in Kentucky during the remainder of 1861.

The naval aspect of the war also began to materialize as 1861 drew to a close. The combined efforts of the Union fleet and army resulted in the fall of a number of key coastal cities in the South. Blockade runners were having little difficulty maintaining the flow of supplies through Lincoln's 'paper blockade,' but it was becoming evident to many that the serious application of the blockade could present a problem which would have far reaching consequences. The disparity between the Union fleet and the Southern naval capabilities made it clear that the future of the naval involvement in the war would be heavily weighted to the Union's advantage.

Early in 1862 Confederate troops in the Virginia area began to harass Union supply and communication lines by attacking points within West Virginia. Those operations were being successfully conducted by Stonewall Jackson. Without warning Jackson was ordered by the Confederate Secretary of War to cease his operations and return to Winchester. Such interference was intolerable to a man of Jackson's character and he promptly resigned his commission. The meddling of politicians in the military affairs of the Confederate army had grown to alarming proportions and the matter was brought to a climax by the incident. Jackson's resignation stirred such controversy in the South that an immediate halt was placed on all direct government interference with combat forces outside the proper channels of the command structure. Jackson was persuaded to return to his command and a valuable lesson was learned by the Confederacy with the least possible harm to the war effort and with the maximum effect on the situation. The Union would learn the same lesson much more slowly and at much greater cost.

Several minor battles, such as the Battle of Mill Springs, occurred in eastern Kentucky in the early weeks of 1862 and resulted in Union victories. In western Kentucky a combined effort by gunboats and ground forces, implemented by Ulysses S Grant and Commodore Andrew Foote, captured the Confederate garrison of Fort Henry on the Tennessee River. Within one week those same Union forces attacked Fort Donelson on the Cumberland River. Confederate attempts to reinforce, defend and counterattack from Fort Donelson failed. Generals John B Floyd and Gideon Pillow fled the fortification and on 16 February 1862 General Simon Buckner surrendered to Grant. The terms of that capitulation, 'Immediate, unconditional surrender,' would become synonymous with General Grant and his concept of total war. The elimination of Fort Donelson combined with Union successes in other areas of Kentucky made it obvious that the state was under Union control. Tennessee was also in a perilous position. There General Albert Sydney Johnston and his Confederate army retired to Murfreesboro in the face of the Union advance. These weeks also saw Union troops and gunboats capture points all along the Mississippi River. A major Union victory had been achieved at Pea Ridge in western Arkansas. Those victories assured Union dominance in Missouri. When coupled with the fall of Kentucky and Union success in Roanoke and New Bern, North Carolina, Kerstown, Virginia, and in Florida it appeared that the Union was destined for a triumphant year.

The war at sea had also opened with a significant action. In March 1862 the CSS *Virginia* (commonly known as the *Merrimack*, the name of the Union vessel from which she was built) and the USS *Monitor* fought the first battle of ironclad vessels. Although the *Virginia* successfully destroyed several Union ships in Chesapeake Bay in the Battle of Hampton Roads, the battle between the two ironclads was technically a stalemate. The engagement served to prove the superior qualities of the Union ironclad construction over the Confederate vessel, an important factor in the future of naval warfare.

Although Union forces had been victorious in the West, the Union command structure was in a state of confusion. McClellan was technically commander of all Union forces, but the various regions and military districts each had their own individual commanders who appeared to be fighting their own private wars without consideration for or cooperation with any other command section. Such a situation was obvious in the West between Major General

Above: 'Stonewall' Jackson earned his nickname at Bull Run.

Henry W Halleck and Brigadier General Don Carlos Buell. Each had his own personal strategy, which involved the other, yet neither was willing to cooperate in the execution of his rival's strategy. Halleck ordered Grant's army of 42,000 to proceed from Fort Donelson along the Tennessee River to Pittsburg Landing and there await further developments. Grant did not accompany his army, which had been placed under the command of Brigadier General CF Smith. Halleck, who was extremely jealous of Grant's military success and expertise, had him arrested after the battle for Fort Donelson on charges of disobeying direct orders, neglect of duty and drunkenness.

During the march of those forces toward Pittsburg Landing the Union command structure was again changed and Halleck was given full charge of operations in the West. He immediately ordered Buell and his 50,000 troops to rendezvous at Pittsburg Landing. At that site General Smith collapsed with a fatal case of tetanus and, as Halleck had no desire to take sole responsibility for the task which lay ahead, he grudgingly dropped his charges and restored Grant to command.

By the end of March Grant had joined his forces at Shiloh, Tennessee. The Union camp stretched around the old Shiloh Meeting House and along the banks of the Tennessee River. The army, sprawled across the countryside, did not concern itself with

Above: the victories gained by Ulysses Grant in the West earned him the command of all the Union armies.

Right: the Union navy captured New Orleans in April 1862.

establishing a defensive position, as it considered the Confederate forces in the area completely demoralized and on the defensive. This was hardly the case. AS Johnston's army had been bolstered by 15,000 troops from the Gulf of Mexico region and 10,000 from Columbus, Kentucky. A Confederate army of more than 40,000 was assembling at Corinth, Mississippee, just across the state border. General PGT Beauregard had joined Johnston as second in command and together they formulated the plans for the impending attack on the Union forces at Shiloh. It was evident that such an attack would have to be made quickly before Buell's army could arrive to reinforce Grant. The Confederate army marched toward Shiloh, intending to attack on the morning of 5 April 1862. Owing to bad weather conditions and the confusion of the march, the attack was delayed until the morning of 6 April. The Union camp lay unsuspect-

ing and, had it not been for pickets of Brigadier General Benjamin Prentiss' Division encountering the Confederate forces, the attack would have come as a complete surprise. In spite of that belated warning, the Union army was caught by the charge of the Confederate infantry before it could properly assemble.

The Confederate army was drawn up in four massive lines with a three-mile front for consecutive attacks on the Union forces. General William J Hardee's Corps led the attack with the corps of General Braxton Bragg, General Polk and finally General John C Breckinridge following. The five Union divisions prepared to defend as best they could. The divisions of Prentiss and Sherman received the full force of the initial assault. Although Sherman stubbornly held his position around Shiloh Church, the raw recruits Prentiss commanded broke almost

immediately before the combined frontal and flank assault. Commanders of the remaining three divisions, Major General Stephen Hurlbut, Major General John A McClernand and Brigadier General WHL Wallace, struggled to organize their forces to reinforce the Union position. Grant, who had been away from the camp awaiting Buell's arrival, rushed back to Shiloh, as yet unaware of the scope of the Confederate offensive. He ordered Major General Lew Wallace's division, which was camped at Crump's Landing some distance from the other five divisions, to make ready his forces as a reserve.

By 0900 hours both Prentiss and Sherman had relinquished their positions. Falling back to a secondary line of defense, Sherman established a defensive stance along the Purdy and Hamburg Road. By 0930 hours the Union forces had established their line. General Hurlbut, with the support of Jeb Stuart, was

on the Union left flank. Prentiss and WHL Wallace has assumed a position along a sunken road and comprised the Union center. McClernand and finally Sherman established the Union right flank. It was imperative that this defense hold until the advance guard of Lew Wallace or Buell could arrive.

The position of the Union defense caused AS Johnston to concentrate his main effort against the forces of Wallace, Prentiss and Hurlbut. Johnston realized that if he could break the Union defense in that area, dubbed 'the Hornet's Nest' by the Confederates, Grant would be forced to abandon the battlefield. From 0930 hours until after 1630 hours the battle raged between the Confederate lines and the Union defenders. Twelve separate Confederate assaults were made and the Hornet's Nest became a scene of mass slaughter. Johnston himself became engrossed in the battle and led seven assaults to dislodge Hurlbut from the area known as the Peach Orchard. During one of those assaults Johnston was wounded in the leg. The apparently minor wound bled unnoticed into his high-topped boots and the general collapsed and was removed from the field. He died from loss of blood at 1430 hours, while the battle continued to rage. Beauregard assumed command and by 1530 hours no less than 60 Confederate artillery pieces had been assembled and trained on the Hornet's Nest.

Both flanks of the Hornet's Nest began to crumble. Stuart's defense had collapsed and Hurlbut's troops were in serious trouble at the Peach Orchard. Wallace, on the Union left, was barely able to keep his position. Grant anticipated the arrival of reinforcements and decided to withdraw to Pittsburg Landing. By 1630 hours Prentiss realized the hopelessness of his situation and he surrendered his 2200 remaining troops. WHL Wallace attempted to make a break from the Hornet's Nest and reach Pittsburg Landing via the ravine of Tillman's Creek. Wallace himself was killed almost immediately and the majority of his remaining forces was massacred when Confederate troops trapped them in the ravine, which received the name 'Hell's Hollow.' However the efforts of Prentiss' and Wallace's divisions bought valuable time for Grant's withdrawal. Confederate forces were stalled for two hours as they waited for ammunition supplies to arrive so that they could pursue the Union army. By the time the Confederates could continue their assault their momentum had been lost and Grant had been able to establish a rapid defense at Pittsburg Landing. Desperate attempts to capture the Union artillery protecting Pittsburg Landing were finally repulsed and, although Bragg ordered an assault on the Union defenses, Beauregard rescinded those orders. Beauregard did not realize that, although the vanguard of Buell's army was arriving, Grant had only 7000 able-bodied men to defend his position. By morning the arrival of Lew Wallace and Buell would swell that number to 25,000 which was 5000 more than Beauregard had at his disposal.

On the morning of 7 April Grant launched an unproductive counterattack. While Grant deliberated his next move, Beauregard, realizing that victory was no longer possible, removed his army from the battlefield. The move shocked the Union command, but General Sherman summarized their relief at the Confederate departure by saying 'We had had quite enough of their society for two days and were glad to be rid of them on any terms.' The Confederate army had chosen to relinquish the field rather than be driven from it. The first major campaign of the Civil War had ended. More than 24,000 men from both armies were killed, wounded or missing, the vast majority of whom died in an area of less than half a square mile at the Hornet's Nest. The battle of Shiloh indicated that a long and bitter struggle lay ahead. It

also forged the Union army in the West into a strong fighting machine and, finally, it opened an avenue to the Mississippi River basin for the Union armies.

After the victory 'Old Brains' Halleck consolidated the independent armies in the West into an army of more than 120,000 men. That army set out for Corinth, Mississippi, but Halleck's inexperience in command and overcautious nature caused the army to move at a snail's pace. After each day's march the army was forced to waste time and energy constructing defenses and it was the end of May before they finally reached their objective. By then Beauregard had long since left the area.

On 7 April Commodore Foote and General John Pope had combined forces to capture Island No 10 on the Mississippi River. After that Union success, Pope's forces joined Halleck's army on the march to Corinth. At the mouth of the Mississippi River, Admiral David G Farragut captured New Orleans, while the Union armies maneuvered. The Mississippi River was open to Union traffic except for the stretch which lay between Vicksburg and Port Hudson. Memphis fell and Chattanooga, Tennessee, was threatened. The Confederate situation in the West was indeed grim.

It was then that Halleck did the incomprehensible. He divided his massive army, scattering its components throughout the western region. The Confederates took full advantage of the situation. During the late summer, the cavalry of Colonels Nathan B Forrest and John H Morgan harassed and destroyed Union supply and communications lines. Major General Kirby Smith won an important battle at Richmond, Kentucky, in mid-August and this served to raise the morale and increase the momentum of the Confederate forces. General Braxton Bragg took command from Beauregard and attempted to capitalize on the victories in Kentucky. Throughout the summer and fall Halleck forfeited all that had been gained at Shiloh. The Confederacy was able to recover and the forces under Grant and Sherman were the only ones to conduct successful operations. The Union victory in the West that Shiloh had appeared to presage degenerated into stalemate.

In the East, after the battle between *Monitor* and *Merrimac*, McClellan concentrated on achieving Lincoln's primary goal, the capture of Richmond. With events favoring the Union in the East, Lincoln and his generals believed that Richmond's capture would result in the collapse of the Confederacy. An attack from the south seemed impossible, so McClellan decided to move the Army of the Potomac to Fort Munroe, Virginia, along the Potomac River to attack the Confederate capital from the east, as that was the direction of least resistance. With Union armies positioned to the west, north and east of Richmond the Confederate command could never be certain from which direction the main attack would come.

McClellan's strategy had several flaws, but the

most important resulted from Lincoln's fear of a Confederate attack on Washington. McClellan could not be swayed from his intended approach to Richmond and Lincoln refused to leave the conventional land approach between Richmond and Washington unprotected. As McClellan prepared to leave Washington, he discovered that he had lost a large part of his intended 150,000-man army, as Lincoln refused to permit the Washington defense army to leave the city. Troops would have to be marched from West Virginia to bolster the capital's defenses before Lincoln would release additional troops to McClellan's Peninsular Campaign. McClellan also lost command of all Union armies when he left the city, because Lincoln considered it impossible to command a field army and the other armies simultaneously. The Union President's displeasure with McClellan's intended campaign was evident.

The plans for the reinforcement of Washington and the subsequent reinforcement of McClellan were brought to nought, largely through the efforts of one man, Stonewall Jackson. Jackson's Shenandoah Valley Campaign was one of the most tactically brilliant and strategically important military operations of modern history. His primary function was to distract Union troops from the Washington defenses and McClellan's campaign. He accomplished that despite the Union's initial troop superiority in the Valley region of more than five to one.

The Shenandoah Valley Campaign began in March 1862 when Major General Nathaniel Banks was ordered to clear the Valley of Confederate forces and proceed to Manassas to defend Washington. As Banks entered the Valley, Jackson steadily withdrew, giving Banks the impression that the Union force had overwhelmed the Confederates. As a result of the lack of Confederate resistance, Banks began moving units of his 20,000-man army toward Washington. Consequently Lincoln released McDowell's Washington defense corps to join McClellan. On 23 March Jackson attacked Banks at Kernstown on the northern edge of the valley. Although the Confederate forces were forced to withdrawn after the day-long battle, Banks was convinced that Jackson would not have attacked without significant reinforcements in the area. Lincoln was similarly convinced and he not only recalled McDowell to Washington, but sent a division to West Virginia to support Banks.

By the beginning of May the positions in the valley region and the peninsula were relatively unchanged and McClellan was anxious to be rid of the threat Jackson posed. The Union command devised a two-pronged attack in the Shenandoah Valley. General Banks was to proceed from the north through the valley, while Union forces in West Virginia, commanded by Major General John C Frémont moved to Staunton at the southern end of the valley. Banks' progress in the valley was so slow that Jackson per-

Above: Jackson's 'Foot Cavalry' dominated the Shenandoah Valley.

ceived the Union intention to crush him between the two forces. After receiving reinforcements, Jackson left a small contingent in Banks' path to maintain his ruse, then embarked his remaining troops on trains allegedly bound for Richmond. His deception convinced even his own troops, who were amazed when they arrived at Staunton. Jackson marched west immediately toward McDowell, Virginia, colliding with Frémont's army en route on 8 May and defeating it. The Confederate pursuit of the Union forces was so aggressive that Frémont managed to escape only by setting the forest on fire in his army's wake.

With Jackson in McDowell, Lincoln felt secure enough to transfer General McDowell's troops to McClellan and Banks began to move north through the valley, sending troops to Washington and toward Richmond. Banks expected future action by Jackson in the valley, but he was taken completely by surprise when on 23 May Union forces were attacked at Front Royal. Banks could not believe that Jackson could march so quickly from his previous position and assumed that another Confederate army was in the valley. Banks immediately withdrew to Winchester where he was again defeated, causing him to retreat across the Potomac River on 25 May. Chaos ensued. McDowell's corps was again recalled and half of it sent to reinforce Banks. The troops which Banks had previously released to Richmond were also recalled and General Frémont was ordered to rendezvous with them at Manassas Gap, east of Front Royal. Every attempt was being made to isolate and destroy Jackson's forces and Jackson's primary function was being accomplished. The Union command congratulated itself on the fact that Jackson's situation was now hopeless and what remained of McDowell's corps set out once more toward Richmond. Jackson astonished them all by attacking Major General James Shields' column as it approached from the east. Jackson had left Ewell's Division to counter Frémont at Cross Keys and with the remainder of his forces defeated Shields at the Battle of Port Republic on 9 June. McDowell was for the last time withdrawn to Washington and the Union forces in the entire Shenandoah Valley area were in complete chaos. The degree of confusion and disorganization was later evidenced by the fact that Jackson was able to slip away from the valley and join in the defense of Richmond, while the Union forces were never able to reinforce McClellan. Jackson had exceeded all expectations and had earned his troops the title 'Foot Cavalry' for their rapid movements up and down the Shenandoah Valley.

While Jackson staged his operations, an important change was made in the Confederate command structure of the army defending Richmond. On 13 May Confederate forces were defeated at the Battle of Seven Pines and their commander, General JE Johnston, was seriously wounded. Confederate President Jefferson Davis made the only logical choice for Johnston's replacement and on 1 June 1862 Robert E Lee, Davis' military advisor, assumed command of the Army of Northern Virginia. Lee immediately began consolidating forces from North and South Carolina and Georgia into his army. He sent Ewell to offer Jackson reinforcements and used Jeb Stuart's cavalry to screen the Army of Northern Virginia's operations and disrupt McClellan's supply and communication lines.

By the end of June the Richmond fortifications had been strengthened and Lee's army stood ready. Jackson was on his way to rendezvous with Lee and, rather than stand in defense against a numerically-superior Union army, Lee decided to take advantage of McClellan's deployment and attack. Brigadier General Fitz-John Porter's Corps was positioned north of the Chickahominy River awaiting reinforcements from McDowell's corps. McClellan's other four corps were south of the river preparing to meet the Confederates. Lee intended to launch an attack on McClellan's army, attacking it piecemeal beginning with Porter's corps.

On 25 June Lee launched his offensive with a frontal assault by General AP Hill's Division against Porter at Mechanicsville. Porter's outlying forces withdrew to the main position behind Beaverdam Creek approximately one mile east of Mechanicsville. On 26 June Hill was forced to wait until late afternoon before continuing his attack. Jackson, who was to join him by making a flank attack on Porter's right, was for the only time in his career late to the battlefield. By the time Hill attacked, Porter had strengthened his defenses and the Confederate forces were repulsed, but Porter began to withdraw. Not only was he facing

Above: Lt Col AV Colburn was McClennan's ADC during the Seven Days' Battle.

Right: Union officers urge their troops forward during Second Manassas.

Hill and Jackson, but Major General James Longstreet's forces were joining the battle near Gaines Mill. Porter was seriously outnumbered but on the night of 27 June he managed to cross the Chickahominy River and begin a march to join the main Union army.

By 28 June McClellan's strategy was shattered by the chaos of the Union supply lines, which was caused by the unexpected Confederate advance. His only option was to withdraw south to the James River, regroup his army there and reestablish his supply route. The final three days of the Seven Days' Battle saw the Battle of Savage's Station on 29 June, the Battle of Frayser's Farm on 30 June, and the Battle of Malvern Hill on 1 July, all of which were little more than rearguard actions by the Union army. However the Confederates were repulsed at each attempt and after a costly fray at Malvern Hill, Lee decided not to continue the pursuit but to return to Richmond. The Seven Days' Battle accomplished several goals. It removed the Union threat to the Confederate capital and restored the confidence of the Army of Northern Virginia. Although Lee had lost nearly 25 percent of his 85,000-man army compared to Union losses of 16,000 out of 100,000, Confederate forces had captured more than 30,000 small arms and 52 cannon. A boost in morale and much-needed weapons were valuable assets to the Confederate armies.

In pursuing McClellan, Lee had left Richmond and most of western Virginia virtually unprotected. Lincoln recognized that fact and consolidated the Shenandoah Valley forces and the Washington defense troops into a new army. He put Major General John Pope in command of that army, which caused Major General Frémont to resign in indignation. Pope immediately set about rebuilding the army in the manner which had brought him success in the West.

The confusion which had reigned during McClellan's Peninsular Campaign and the Shenandoah Valley incidents convinced Lincoln that the armies required a general in chief. He again chose a commander from the West, putting Halleck in the position. Halleck, who had ridden the wave of success on the military skills of his subordinates, was not the man for the task. He concentrated too heavily on the importance of cities and geographic locations. While Pope organized his army near Culpeper, Virginia, Halleck ordered McClellan to return to Washington to join Pope. Had Halleck taken the time to survey the situation he would have realized that the Army of Northern Virginia was trapped between Pope and McClellan. A strong, coordinated effort would certainly have resulted in a Union victory and perhaps the fall of Richmond.

When Lee realized that McClellan was leaving the Virginia peninsula he was free to focus his attention on Pope's army. In early August Lee advanced 24,000 men commanded by Stonewall Jackson to Gordonsville. Jackson then struck north and defeated elements of Pope's army at Cedar Mountain. Pope was not overly concerned as he knew that Jackson was no match for his Union force of 45,000. Unknown to Pope, Lee was on the march from Richmond with more than 30,000 troops to rendezvous with Jackson. Lee intended to surprise Pope and defeat him, which would create havoc with the Union command's strategies. However Lee's chances for success were removed when a minor cavalry skirmish occurred. Although Jeb Stuart narrowly escaped being taken prisoner, a copy of Lee's orders was captured by the Union cavalry. Those orders demonstrated the weakness of Pope's position against the massing Confederate army and he immediately retreated north across the Rap-

pahannock River. McClellan's army, which had been returning up the Potomac River, disembarked at Fredericksburg and Alexandria and set out immediately to join Pope's forces. However Pope, apparently convinced that he held a strong position, refused to move toward those reinforcements. It was then that Stuart claimed his revenge for the loss of Lee's battle plans, when his troopers managed to capture a copy of Pope's orders. Lee had realized that the arrival of McClellan would mean a Union superiority, but the orders indicated that Pope's force would swell to more than 100,000 within two days, against a Confederate force of 54,000.

Lee had to act quickly if he hoped to defeat Pope. He devised a plan which divided his army into two parts, half commanded by Jackson and half under Lee's personal command. He intended to send Jackson on a wide sweep around Pope's right flank to attack the Union rear, while Lee's force swung around the left flank. Pope would react to Jackson's maneuver and then Lee would reunite his army to crush the Union force. On 25 August Jackson set out and by the following day his troops had marched more than 60 miles to Bristow. There the Confederate troops discovered a supply depot from which they confiscated food, clothing and equipment that they had long been lacking. Later the same day Lee began his maneuver. By 27 August Jackson was in Manassas and Pope smugly believed that Lee had made a grave error in tactics. Rather than retreat, Pope decided to isolate and destroy Jackson's small army then turn and destroy Lee. That was exactly what Lee had hoped he would do.

Pope moved toward Manassas, but was then informed that Jackson had been seen in Centreville, five miles north of Manassas. Pope changed course for

Centreville, only to have Jackson evade him again. Finally Jackson revealed his position at Groveton by attacking Pope's forces as they marched late in the evening of 28 August. Jackson definitely had the advantage. Pope's forces were disorganized and wearied by the march and countermarch in search of the Confederate troops. Jackson had drawn Pope to a battlefield of his own choosing and, by the initial reaction of the Union commander, Jackson was convinced that Pope believed the Confederate forces to be in retreat. McClellan's advancing army was drawing near, but Jackson's task was to keep Pope in position until Lee could arrive.

On the morning of 29 August Pope made tentative attacks against the Confederate position, which lay on what had been the westernmost boundary of the First Battle of Manassas, expecting Jackson to withdraw and begin the cat and mouse chase game once again. In the face of Confederate resistance, Pope decided to launch an assault against the Confederate right flank. That Union attack, commanded by Major General Fitz-John Porter, was brought to an abrupt halt by the appearance of Lee's forces directly in the path of the intended attack. Porter realized that he was outnumbered and took a defensive stance which forced the situation into a stalemate. The following day Pope ordered an attack just north of the Warrenton Turnpike. Although the Union troops made numerous attempts to break the Confederate line, the musket and artillery fire brought to bear against them was devastating. That degree of rifle fire could not be maintained indefinitely and Jackson's troops had soon exhausted their ammunition supplies. The Union forces then launched a final attack to carry the position, but they were met by the arrival of Longstreet's Corps of fresh troops. The attack was repulsed and Longstreet realized that the Union left flank had been exposed. He advanced to capture Bald Hill, the scene of bitter fighting during the First Battle of Manassas. Pope saw that his avenue of retreat was being blocked and rushed troops from all sectors of the front toward Henry House Hill. Jackson took full advantage of the weakened Union front and attacked, forcing Pope to fall back, until Union forces were safely behind the Washington defenses.

The Second Battle of Manassas was another Confederate victory. General Porter became Pope's scapegoat for the failure of the operation, despite the fact that Porter had in fact acted wisely. Of the 70,000 Union troops in the area approximately 60,000 actually participated in the battle and more than 14,000 of them became casualties or were taken prisoner. Lee had employed all of his forces with losses of less than 10,000 men, but he had succeeded in capturing thousands of small arms and at least 30 cannon. The morale of the army of Northern Virginia soared and Lee put his plans for an invasion of the North into operation. An attack on Washington was not a viable option, as the armies of both Pope and McClellan were concentrated in that area. In view of the recent favorable events, Lee decided that a successful attack on Northern soil could have far-reaching consequences. European nations, particularly Britain and France, would be impressed by such a victory and would increase their support of the Confederate cause. Lee also hoped to add fuel to the Northern Peace Movement's campaign against the war. Not least of all, there were supplies and materiels in the North which would greatly enhance the Confederate arsenals.

Lee acted immediately and crossed the Potomac River at a point between Leesburg, Virginia, and Martinsburg, Maryland, with his 55,000 men. From there, with Jackson's troops leading the army, Lee moved toward Frederick, Maryland. On 9 September Lee issued Special Order 191, his battle plan for the impending campaign. This order divided the army into four parts. Three of those forces were to take different routes and then converge on Harper's Ferry. The fourth would march westward across South Mountain. In dividing his army, Lee demonstrated that he had little to fear of the threat McClellan's army posed in the area. This assurance would have been well founded, except for the fact that on the night of 13 September Union troops discovered a copy of Special Order 191 wrapped around a bundle of cigars at a Confederate campsite. Through those orders McClellan realized that the movement of the Confederate forces across South Mountain was dependent on the access route through Turner's Gap and that the gap must be secured. Yet, true to his nature, rather than send forces immediately to the gap McClellan waited until morning before acting. This procrastination was a serious mistake as Jeb Stuart informed Lee of the probability that a copy of the Speical Order had been captured. Lee immediately sent troops to secure the area.

On 14 September Major General Burnside's forces were engaged by defensively positioned Confederate troops in the Battle of Turner's Gap. Further south at Crampton's Gap Confederate troops attempted to block Major General William Franklin's forces. The battles raged throughout the day but by night both Burnside and Franklin had broken through the gaps. It was obvious that Lee's 19,000-man segment of the Army of Northern Virginia was no match for the 90,000 men at McClellan's disposal and he retreated toward Sharpsburg, Maryland. Lee was concerned about the mission at Harper's Ferry, but on reaching Sharpsburg he received word from Jackson that the garrison of more than 10,000 Union troops had been captured. Jackson further informed Lee that his forces would set out immediately to rendezvous at Sharpsburg. Had McClellan attacked Lee on 15 September the overwhelmingly superior numbers of the Union army

Above: the Battle of Antietam opened with a flank attack on the Confederate Army by 'Fightin' Joe' Hooker's Corps.

would certainly have destroyed Lee's forces. Instead McClellan paused once again, waiting until 17 September before initiating his assault. By that time Jackson's forces had arrived from Harper's Ferry, increasing the Confederate army's numbers to more than 40,000, and Lee had maneuvered his troops into a defensive position.

The wisdom of Lee's defense has often been questioned. He faced a Union force twice the size of his own army, yet Lee chose to position his troops with their backs to the Potomac River, which was only three miles away. His right flank lay behind Antietam Creek, an easily-fordable stream. His left flank was located north of Sharpsburg in a wooded area on the Hagerstown Road. Neither area provided a strong defensive position. The center lines of the Army of Northern Virginia stretched over two miles of rolling hills and farmland. Only the artillery, stationed at a higher elevation overlooking the battle area, had a strong position. Lee's tactics at the impending Battle of Antietam appeared to revolve around the personality of his opponent and McClellan's apparent inability to follow through with a coordinated attack.

After cautiously maneuvering his forces, McClellan launched an attack on the Confederate left flank with Major General 'Fightin' Joe' Hooker's Corps at 0600 hours on 17 September. The battle there raged for more than one hour, but the Confederate forces of Brigadier General Jubal Early and Major General John B Hood held their position. Hooker's exhausted troops were repulsed, but the attack was renewed at a new point by Major General Joseph K Mansfield's Corps. As the weary Confederate line gave way, Union forces drove forward toward Dunkard Church. General Mansfield was slain but the battle continued for more than 30 minutes. The situation at Dunkard Church was critical and Confederate troops were shifted from the right flank to reinforce the sector, while Confederate artillery continued its bombardment of the Union advance. At 0900 hours a division of Major General Edwin Sumner's Corps launched the third wave of the Union attack to capture Dunkard Church. That attack would have succeeded had not Major General Lafayette McLaws' division arrived at precisely that moment to reinforce the Confederate lines. The Union assault lost momentum and the Confederate left flank was locked in stalemate.

The remainder of Sumner's Corps was prepared to strike the Confederate center line. Although Daniel Harvey Hill's forces had taken a position along a sunken road, the Union attack was so intense that it finally succeeded in flanking the road. The confused orders of a wounded officer caused the Confederate forces to panic. 'Bloody Lane' as it was to become known, was a scene of mass confusion as the Confederate troops fell back. Had the Union forces pursued their advantage, Lee's army would have been split into two parts. However the intensity of the fighting had taken its toll and the attackers had lost their momentum and cohesion. Without a Union follow through, General DH Hill's troops were able to retreat from the area.

Burnside's corps was to cross Antietam Creek on the Confederate right flank and advance to Sharpsburg, thereby blocking Lee's avenue of retreat. Rather than ford the creek, Burnside battled to capture a small bridge. His repeated attempts to perform that task continued throughout the morning until the bridge was finally taken at 1300 hours. Burnside then spent more than two hours consolidating his forces on the Confederate side of the creek before initiating his advance. At 1600 hours Burnside arrived at Sharpsburg, but his ridiculous delays had given General AP Hill's Light Division an opportunity to reach the battlefield from Harper's Ferry. Hill's forces swept Burnside's flank and forced him to retreat back to Antietam Creek.

The Battle of Antietam was virtually ended. Lee refused to remove his army from the battlefield, accurately assessing McClellan's character yet again. Although the Army of Northern Virginia remained in position throughout 18 September, no Union attack was forthcoming and that night Lee safely withdrew across the Potomac River. The cost to both armies in one day's fighting was phenomenal. Lee had 40,000 troops at the opening of the battle, of which more than 25 percent were killed, wounded or missing. Although McClellan had an army of more than 70,000, he had only committed 46,000 troops to the battle. Of that number more than 12,000 were listed as casualties. Although Lee's first invasion of the North had been reversed he had not actually lost the battle; he merely retreated to reformulate his strategy and reorganize his army.

During Lee's invasion in the East, General Bragg initiated his own invasion of Kentucky. This attempt was brought to a halt on 8 October at the Battle of Perryville. Although Bragg could claim a nominal victory, he had insufficient men and equipment to pursue the invasion. While in the East and West the situation was precariously balanced, with neither side able to claim resounding victories attention was again drawn to the Mississippi River region. The point was emphasized that the capture of the river by Union forces would divide the Confederacy in half. General Grant focussed his attention on Vicksburg, the primary stumbling block to Union possession of the river. He initiated his campaign to capture Vicksburg by dividing his army in half, one part commanded by Sherman and the other under his own command. Sherman's forces were to travel down the Mississippi, landing one mile north of Vicksburg. Grant intended to move overland to unite with Sherman and attack the Confederate city and its garrison. Although the Union command wanted Vicksburg captured, Grant's efforts to do so received only the minimum of support and encouragement. The truth was that, although he was attempting to win the war, politicians and military advisors in Washington were interfering with the war effort for their personal gratification.

Finally on 29 December 1862 Sherman landed at Chickasaw Bluff, where his forces were promptly defeated by waiting Confederate forces. Grant's land force was being harassed by Confederate cavalry, led in part by General Nathan B Forrest, who had succeeded in severing Grant's supply lines. Both Grant and Sherman were forced to retreat, abandoning the hope of capturing Vicksburg in 1862.

In the relative calm after Antietam, while the main war effort was focussed in the western regions, Lee reorganized his army and by December he was again prepared to give battle. Stuart played an active role during those months of stalemate, raiding Union supply and communications lines as far north as Pennsylvania, promoting chaos and panic in both military and civilian quarters. After Lee's first invasion was repulsed Lincoln issued the Emancipation Proclamation and urged McClellan to strike immediately at the Army of Northern Virginia. McClellan had many stuanch political friends, but his failure to act angered the Union President. Finally at the end of October McClellan crossed the Potomac, but he persistently refused to engage Lee's army. Lincoln could no longer tolerate McClellan's unwillingness to pursue the enemy and replaced him with General AE Burnside. Although Burnside would later be criticized for the method of his attack at Fredericksburg, he did in fact attempt to refuse his appointment as commander of the Army of the Potomac, knowing the position to be beyond his capabilities. Lincoln would neither reconsider nor accept Burnside's hesitancy as anything more than an excess of modesty.

Burnside immediately set about engaging the Confederate army. He devised a plan to attack and capture Fredericksburg and from there to launch an offensive against Richmond. The plan of the attack had one principal stumbling block. The Rappahannock River lay below Fredericksburg between the Union and Confederate armies. Burnside had to cross the river and capture the plateau above the city before Lee could escape. Pontoon bridges were therefore ordered for the crossing and, although the Rappahannock could have been forded when the Union forces first arrived, Burnside chose to wait for the bridging equipment. The delay gave Lee the time he needed to prepare his defenses. He placed Longstreet's Corps on the easily defended position of Marye's Heights, the Confederate left flank. Jackson's Corps was positioned on the right flank. Confederate artillery was dispersed along the plateau behind the city for maximum effect and one lone brigade was stationed within Fredericksburg. The Army of

Above: George Meade commanded a division at Fredericksburg.

Northern Virginia had increased to 78,000 men in the preceding months and those troops stood ready for the Union attack.

As his forces arrived, Burnside divided his army of 120,000 men into three Grand Divisions. General Sumner was given command of the Union right flank. Major General Franklin was to cross the Rappahannock on the Union far left and General Hooker was given command of the third Grand Division, which was to wait on the Union side of the river as a reserve. The Union artillery remained with Hooker, placed on the high ground which commanded the entire battleground. On the morning of 11 December Burnside ordered the crossing of the Rappahannock. Franklin's forces proceeded with little difficulty but Sumner's engineers were harassed and impeded by the Confederate skirmishers from within the city. Rather than begin by crossing the river with a small force to disperse the Confederate riflemen, Burnside employed his artillery and the crossing was achieved on the evening of 12 December.

The following morning Burnside altered his plans and, instead of attacking Jackson's position with Franklin's entire force, he sent General George Meade's division forward with two other divisions in support. A dense fog blanketed the battlefield and when it lifted, the Confederate far right flank was surprised by the sight of the advanced Union forces. As they attempted to form a defense, a young horse artillery officer, Major John Pelham, galloped his guns ahead of the Confederate line to engage the Union forces and artillery. For 30 minutes, while the Confederate infantry organized, he kept the Union advance at bay. With his ammunition supply nearly exhausted, Pelham ceased his barrage and galloped his artillery to the safety of the Confederate line. The Union advance continued and Jackson began a

barrage with his own artillery that resulted in a one and a half hour artillery duel with the Union guns. The Confederate artillery was finally silenced and the Union advance resumed. Meade attacked, breaching the Confederate line, only to find that his support divisions had failed to move with him. Without that support, the Confederate counterattack drove Meade's forces back to their original positions. Although they attempted to pursue, the Confederate troops could make no further advance beyond their original lines of defense.

On the Confederate left flank Sumner, supported by Hooker, assaulted Marye's Heights. In 14 separate attacks the Union forces were never able to get closer than 25 yards to the stone wall behind which the Confederate troops had laid their defense. Although the Union soldiers threw themselves at the defenses, the situation was hopeless. The elevation of the Confederate position was simply too great a handicap. As evening approached they withdrew to consolidate below the heights.

Burnside ordered renewed attacks on the morning of 14 December, but the army was exhausted and demoralized. His generals were incredulous at his intention to continue the wholesale slaughter of their men and eventually they convinced him that it was pointless to resume the attack. Two days later, after minor skirmishing, the Army of the Potomac withdrew across the Rappahannock. Union losses at Fredericksburg were more than 12,600, of which nearly 12,000 were incurred at Marye's Heights. Lee lost approximately 5300 men. Although Fredericksburg was considered a resounding Confederate victory, Lee could have made the result more decisive if he had counterattacked Bragg's army while it lay between the heights and the river.

On 31 December Bragg's Army of Tennessee and Major General William Rosecrans' Army of the Cumberland clashed at the Battle of Murfreesboro in Tennessee. Although Bragg was considered victorious, both he and Rosecrans suffered 25 percent casualties in the battle and it was Bragg who decided to withdraw from the city. The Union forces lost a great deal of confidence and a large quantity of arms and artillery pieces, but they retained possession of Murfreesboro. A young Brigadier General, Philip H Sheridan, who would play a key role in the latter years of the war, was responsible for saving the Army of the Cumberland from total defeat.

As 1862 drew to a close the opposing armies sought winter quarters. The Confederate armies had maintained the status quo and the Confederate government was satisfied with the turn of events. Lincoln was saddled with a demoralized eastern army and the failure of his generals to accomplish substantial victories on almost every front. It was fortunate for all parties that winter had arrived. They could consolidate and formulate strategies for the new year.

3 THE UNION GATHERS STRENGTH

Far left: Allan Pinkerton (left) pictured with Lincoln and General McClernand. His detective agency's intelligence-gathering was ineffective.
Left: 'Fightin' Joe' Hooker became commander of the Army of the Potomac in January 1863.
Right: Confederate troops advance on Cemetery Ridge during the Battle of Gettysburg.

In the early winter months of 1863 there seemed to be a chance that the United States of America would remain divided into two nations. The Confederate armies had succeeded in maintaining the integrity of the Confederate States and European support was increasing. Preserving the Union had not been as simple as the North had originally believed and the Southern states were defiantly refusing to be brought back into line. The voice of the Northern Peace Movement grew louder. The year 1863 was to be decisive for both the North and South. If the South could remain victorious the North would surely sue for peace. If the North could gain a dominant position the South would begin to suffer the attrition of war.

The first task facing the Union command was the replacement of General Burnside. Although several eligible candidates were considered, Major General Joseph Hooker was the most politically influential and in January 1863 he became the new commander of the Army of the Potomac. Hooker immediately set about reorganizing the army. There were several months ahead before spring would bring the armies together again. With morale as a key factor, Hooker implemented a furlough system to alleviate the tedium of the war. He also instituted an extensive training program of mock battles, which improved not only the soldiers' techniques but also the efficiency of their officers. The corps themselves were reorganized into individual self-contained entities. Hooker dismissed the ineffectual Pinkerton Agency and developed his own intelligence-gathering system, commanded by Colonel

Sharp. The self-confidence and strength of the Army of the Potomac grew. However the organizational and administrative qualities Hooker possessed would be cast into the shadows by his conceited, over-confident nature when his army was at last put to the test.

Along the Eastern and Gulf Coasts the Union blockade was becoming increasingly effective. Grant was working closely with Admiral David Porter on plans for a second campaign against Vicksburg in the West. On all fronts Confederate cavalry was harassing and embarrassing Union forces. Captain John S Mosby conducted a daring raid near Washington and Nathan Forrest captured more than 1600 Union troops with a cavalry force of less than 500 men. The condition of Lee's army, which had maintained its position at Fredericksburg, was deteriorating. Supplies of food, clothing, arms and equipment were beginning to suffer through the prolonged effects of the conflict. It was for that reason that Lee chose to remain in his strong defensible position. Lee recognized the effects of a war of attrition and from Fredericksburg he sought a victory which could end the war.

By April the Army of the Potomac had reached an unprecedented strength of 134,000 men and Hooker was prepared to initiate his tactics for the isolation and defeat of the 60,000 troops of the Army of Northern Virginia. Hooker was convinced that the execution of his army's maneuvers would force Lee to react in one of two ways. Either he would retreat to

Richmond, or he would hold his ground and be crushed by overwhelmingly superior numbers. Hooker's battle plan was divided into two principal phases. First he would begin with cavalry raids, commanded by General George Stoneman, to disrupt Confederate supplies from Richmond to Fredericksburg. The second phase would begin with Hooker sending Meade's V Corps, Howard's XI Corps, and Slocum's XII Corps wide around Lee's northern flank for an attack on the Confederate rear. Then Couch's II Corps, Sickles' III Corps and Sedgwick's VI Corps

north. Convinced that this was the true attack, yet unwilling to commit himself fully to a defense in that area, Lee sent Major Richard H Anderson's Division to a rear position near Chancellorsville. Although Jackson urged an attack against Sedgwick's Corps, Lee declined and on 30 April his assessment of the situation proved correct when three Union corps were reported crossing Germanna Ford and Ely's Ford en route for the crossroads at Chancellorsville. Hooker had taken personal command of those forces, satisfied despite the reduction in his cavalry force that

would cross the Rappahannock River in a maneuver to convince Lee that Hooker intended to attack the area around Marye's Heights as Burnside had done. When the flanking corps crossed Germanna and Ely's Fords on the Rapidan River the II and III Corps would move from their position to join the attack on the Confederate rear. Sedgwick would remain at Fredericksburg to threaten Lee's army from a frontal position.

On 13 April Hooker ordered Stoneman to begin his raids. However severe storms swelled the Rappahannock, leaving one cavalry brigade trapped on the Confederate side of the river and delaying the cavalry action for a full 14 days. Hooker chose to adhere to his original timetable in spite of this setback and began the flanking maneuvers of the V, XI, and XII Corps on 27 April. On 28 April these corps crossed the Rappahannock at Kelly's Ford. On the morning of 29 April Sedgwick crossed the Rappahannock below the heights of Fredericksburg. Lee looked on, unable to believe that Hooker intended to repeat Burnside's December performance. That night Lee received information about Union activity to the

all was proceeding as planned. The activity on the Fredericksburg to Richmond railroad convinced Hooker that Lee had chosen to retreat. After a brief skirmish with Anderson's forces, which forced the Confederates to retreat, Hooker decided to halt his advance at Chancellorsville to regroup and consolidate his army.

Lee was surprised by Hooker's sudden halt, but decided to use it to his own advantage. He discarded the idea of retreat, realizing that it could not be accomplished without a high percentage of casualties. With Stonewall Jackson's aid, Lee formulated a counteroffensive. It would be difficult as the element of surprise was crucial, and Jackson alone could accomplish the task. Lee decided to keep General Jubal Early's Division at Fredericksburg to counterbalance Sedgwick's threat and a minimal force at his own command. He gave Jackson the command of the remaining available forces for a surprise attack on Hooker's right flank. Jackson was faced with a march across the front of Hooker's army to the area known as the Wilderness, a sector of thick forest growth, without alerting the Union forces.

Jackson began his march on the morning of 2 May with Fitzhugh Lee's cavalry screening the infantry. It was a march of more than 15 miles, south to Catherine's Furnace then north on the Brock Road to the Wilderness. At Catherine's Furnace the Confederate force was detected and shots were exchanged. Jackson was convinced that the element of surprise had been lost, but he rapidly continued on his course. In fact Hooker was apprised of the encounter, but despite the arguments of his staff he refused to believe that it was anything more than a Confederate ploy to cover their retreat. In those hours Hooker made several fatal errors in judgment which can be directly attributed to his conceit. He ignored the implications of Confederate activity as he believed that his position, particularly on the right flank bordering the 'impenetrable' Wilderness, to be impregnable. Also he refused to react to the Confederate movement that evening, preferring to deal with it in the broad daylight of the following day.

Jackson's forces reached the Wilderness at approximately 1700 hours on the evening of 2 May. Concerned that his attack was anticipated, Jackson quickly formed his troops and before 1730 hours launched the first wave of his attack. The Union forces were taken completely by surprise as the Confederate troops burst through the Wilderness. The mass of screaming, firing Confederates created chaos in the unprepared Union camp and this quickly gave way to panic and uncontrollable rout. The right flank crumpled as Union troops fled from the area, but darkness had fallen and Jackson's forces were disorganized and losing momentum. The situation had caused both armies to become disoriented and rumors spread through the Confederate lines that Union cavalry was preparing for a counterattack. Jackson decided that if he was to reach his objective at the US Ford Road he would have to assess the situation personally. Ordering his officers to regroup their units, Jackson and his staff rode ahead of the lines directly into a small contingent of Union troops, who fired on them, killing several of Jackson's staff. Himself wounded, Jackson ordered an immediate return to their own lines. Tragically the Confederate infantry upon hearing horses approaching assumed that Union cavalry was attacking and fired on Jackson's returning party. Several more of the staff were killed and Jackson was again wounded. General AP Hill arrived on the scene as Union artillery fired on the Confederate position. Hill and members of his staff joined the growing number of wounded officers. As they were all removed from the field the command of the Confederate forces fell to Major General Robert Rodes. He in turn relinquished command to the more experienced Jeb Stuart. Although the Union forces had been routed, the situation on the Confederate side was one of mass confusion.

On 3 May the Confederate forces continued their assault, but with far less vigor. The events of the previous day had taken their toll and the weary troops faced the stiff resistance of a reorganized Union defense. The Confederate command was therefore astonished when Hooker's army began to retreat. The Union general, who many have claimed was dazed by the explosion of an artillery shell at his headquarters, ordered the retreat of his army. Unable to accept that he had made a seriour error in judgment, Hooker was convinced that Jackson's forces were in fact a second Confederate army arriving at Chancellorsville. Lee's small contingent, which had attacked the Union left flank at the same time as Jackson attacked the right, unsuccessfully attempted to stop Hooker from retreating across the Rappahannock. Hooker then ordered Sedgwick to attack Early's Division at Marye's Heights in an effort to draw Lee's attention from the fleeing corps. Lee reversed the direction of his army to counter Sedgwick. After brief skirmishing between the Union Sixth Corps and the divisions of McLaws and Anderson, Sedgwick turned and withdrew across the river on 4 May. Frustrated by his failure to catch and defeat Sedgwick, Lee again reversed course to pursue Hooker. That march and countermarch, coupled with the events of 2 and 3 May, had exhausted the Army of Northern Virginia. The Army of the Potomac escaped and by the evening of 5 May Lee was in complete controle of the entire Fredericksburg-Chancellorsville area west of the Rappahannock.

Although victorious at the Battle of Chancellorsville, the Confederate army had suffered badly. Not only had some 13,000 casualties been sustained but also Jackson died several days later of pneumonic complications. Union casualties were more than 17,000, but Hooker rather than the Army of the Potomac had been defeated. The unwarranted retreat demoralized the army once again and forced Lincoln to contemplate replacing the commander of his main eastern army for the fifth time.

One month later in the first week of June the reinforced 70,000-man Army of Northern Virginia was marching toward Culpeper, Virginia. The army had been divided into three corps: General James Longstreet's I Corps, General Richard S Ewell's II Corps and General AP Hill's III Corps. Jefferson Davis was anxious for Lee to begin another invasion of the North. Not only was the political and military climate right for such a strategy, but the diminishing Confederate stores of equipment and supplies could be supplemented by the capture of Union stockpiles in the North. Hooker had been ordered to maintain a loose contact with Lee's army, positioning the Army of the Potomac between Lee and Washington, and on 9 June a brief though important skirmish occurred between Union and Confederate cavalry at Brandy Station, Virginia. For the first time in the war Union

Right: aspects of the Battle of Gettysburg painted in 1884.

cavalry performed well against Jeb Stuart's troopers.

On 13 June Ewell's Second Corps reached Winchester, Virginia, and two days later defeated a Union contingent, capturing arms and equipment, including 25 cannon. The army pressed north and Lee ordered Stuart to protect the passes which were essential to the movement of the army through the Blue Ridge Mountains, to act as a screening force and to harass the Union army whenever possible. After Brandy Station the Southern press had severely criticized Stuart's actions, questioning his capabilities as a commander. Lee's inexplicit orders gave Stuart the margin he needed to wage his personal war and on 25 June he set out to redeem his injured pride and integrity. Leaving two cavalry brigades behind to execute Lee's immediate orders, Stuart took three brigades on raiding missions against Union lines and depots. Stuart's exploits would rob Lee of his primary means of intelligence gathering and a large portion of his cavalry at a most critical time.

By 28 June Ewell's Corps had reached Pennsylvania. His corps was divided into two columns, one of which captured Carlisle and advanced on Harrisburg, while the other captured York and Wrightsville. At the same time the 100,000-strong Army of the Potomac parallelled the movement of Lee's forces, reaching Frederick, Maryland, on 28 June. Only as a direct result of Stuart's absence did Lee learn the actual position of the Union army and that Major General George Gordon Meade had replaced Hooker as its commander. At last Lincoln had found a man of military skill and integrity to command his army. Unlike his predecessors, Meade's primary concern was for his men and his duty.

Both Lee and Meade were deprived of their intelligence sources – Lee by Stuart's absence and Meade by the loss of Hooker's personal spy network – as they moved virtually blind toward a battle of major significance. On 30 June a brigade from Hill's Corps moved along the Chambersburg Pike to raid a supply depot in Gettysburg and encountered a division of Union cavalry, which had been sent on a reconnaissance mission in the area. The encounter was reported to the respective army commanders. Lee reacted by ordering Longstreet's Corps at Chambersburg and Ewell's Corps at York to concentrate their forces at Cashtown. Meade, who had been preparing a defensive position at Big Pipe Creek, ordered his III Corps to Emitsburg and his I and II Corps to move northeast toward the Pennsylvania border. Meade and his headquarters remained near Taneytown, a full day's march from the position of his lead divisions.

On the morning of 1 July Brigadier General John Buford's cavalry division had reached Gettysburg and was reconnoitering the area. Buford was uneasy after the encounter with Confederate forces on the previous day and he had received assurances from Major General John F Reynolds, commander of the Union I Corps, that reinforcements would be sent if an engagement with the enemy developed. Major General Henry Heth, commanding a division of Hill's Corps, had received similar assurances from his superiors when he set out along the Chambersburg Pike to reconnoiter and again attempt to secure the supply depot at Gettysburg. Contact was made between the opposing divisions and for more than one and a half hours Buford's dismounted troopers, dispersed

Left: Union forces lost 23,000 men at Gettysburg, compared with over 30,000 Confederate casualties during the battle. Right: a section of the exposed Union position known as the Devil's Den.

along McPherson's Ridge, the Mummasburg Road and Herr Ridge, fought desperately to maintain their positions until infantry reinforcements could arrive. By 0930 hours Reynold's Corps was marching in support and at 1000 hours Major General Abner Doubleday's First Division had reached Marsh Creek. AP Hill was responding by moving a division toward Heth's position and Ewell's Corps was approaching from the north-east.

As the engagement intensified Reynolds requested aid from Major General Oliver O Howard's XI Corps. Minutes later Reynolds met his death at McPherson's Ridge. Doubleday, as the ranking officer at the site of battle, assumed command and in a short time his indecisiveness had brought the Union forces to the brink of collapse. General Howard revived the situation when he rushed forward to relieve Doubleday. As the XI Corps arrived the Confederate forces responded first with an artillery barrage then with an unsuccessful attack by General Rode's division against the stiff resistance of the Union flank north of Gettysburg. Finally Early's division joined that attack turning the Union right flank. Heth had also renewed his attack on the Union I Corps northeast of Gettysburg and, when joined by Major General W Dorsey Pender's Division, that flank was also turned. The Union forces then withdrew from the area to Cemetery Ridge, leaving the Confederate forces in possession of the town and Seminary Ridge. The events which followed typified the manner in which Gettysburg would be lost by the Army of Northern Virginia. Lee ordered Ewell to attack and secure Cemetery Ridge 'if at all possible,' believing that Ewell would make every effort to do so. However

Ewell reviewed the situation, his losses, the disorganization of his units and his need for consolidation and decided that it was not at that time possible. When Ewell finally did send forces to Culp's Hill they were reconnaissance troops which were easily repulsed by the then-organized Union defenders.

News of the first day's fighting reached Meade and he immediately sent Major General Winfield Hancock to Gettysburg to take command of the situation, pending the arrival of Meade himself. By 0100 hours on 2 July Meade had arrived to survey the battlefield. He believed that Cemetery Ridge was a strong defensible position and was convinced that if the Union troops present, almost 75 percent of his total army, could maintain resistance until the remaining forces arrived, the Army of the Potomac would be able to defend its position. In those early hours of 2 July, Lee met with Ewell and Longstreet to outline his plans. He was disappointed that Ewell had not pursued his initial assault, but drew an offensive tactical battle plan for the attack of Cemetery Ridge. Lee continued to believe that the Union flanks were the weakest points in their defense and ordered Ewell to renew his attack on the Union right while Longstreet was to attack the Union left flank. While Ewell's attack distracted the Union forces, Longstreet's objective was to turn the left flank and threaten Meade's rear area. AP Hill's Corps was to maintain a frontal position, employing artillery and keeping the center lines immobilized. Neither Ewell nor Longstreet agreed with Lee's plan. They believed that Lee should maintain the Confederate position on Seminary Ridge and provoke Meade to take the offensive. Lee was not disuaded and the disagreement was

29

reflected in the performance of his generals.

The flank attacks were scheduled to begin simultaneously after dawn on 2 July, but Longstreet's assault did not begin until after 1400 hours. This gave Meade time to disperse his army from Culp's and Cemetery Hills in the north, along Cemetery Ridge and south to the hill known as Little Round Top. Major General Daniel Sickles' III Corps was ordered to the Little Round Top, but after surveying the land Sickles decided that there was a more defensible position along the Emmitsburg Road in an area known as the Peach Orchard. Sickles' unauthorized maneuver left the Little Round Top unprotected and his own corps dangerously exposed as Longstreet's advance began. Meade was furious and rode forward to reprimand Sickles. The Third Corps was forced to remain at its precarious position and, had it not been for the heroic efforts of Major General GK Warren and elements of Major General George Sykes' Fifth Corps, the crucial Little Round Top would have easily been taken by Hood's advancing division.

McLaws' and Anderson's divisions attacked Sickles' forces and swiftly drove them back from the Peach Orchard and nearby Wheatfield. Sickles' corps was more than one mile in front of the Union lines and was on the verge of destruction when the veteran

First Minnesota Infantry Regiment arrived and charged forward to block the Confederate advance. That effort cost the regiment more than 80 percent casualties, but it was successful enough to allow Meade to shift reinforcements from his right flank to bolster the left. The strength of the charge and the arrival of fresh Union troops put a swift halt to Longstreet's advance. Meade would not have been able to maneuver those reinforcements from the right if Ewell had attacked. In fact it was early evening before he sent his troops piecemeal against Culp's and Cemetery Hills. Reportedly the stump of his leg, which had been amputated before the Second Battle of Manassas, was inflamed, but whatever the reason Ewell's failure to initiate his attacks cost the Army of Northern Virginia dearly.

Losses in the first two days of the battle were staggering, but the armies prepared for yet another day of fighting. Meade held a council with his generals on the night of 2 July and although plans for a retreat had been drafted, the assurances given by his generals persuaded Meade to maintain his position for at least one more day. Meade then reviewed the situation and decided that, as Lee had already tried his flanks, the Confederate assault would resume against the Union center. Meade consequently reinforced this area with

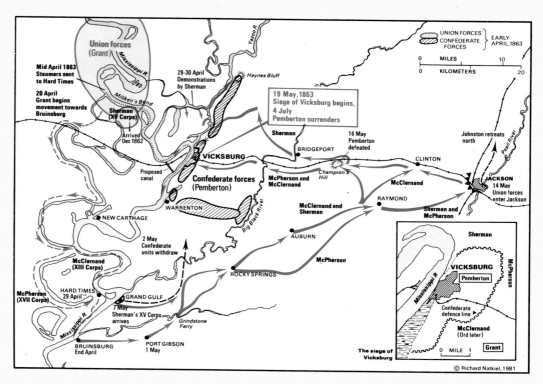

men and artillery. Lee too held council with his generals. Although exceptionally astute at strategic planning, Lee obviously missed Jackson's tactical expertise. He decided that the threats to the Union flanks had weakened the Union center and chose to attack precisely where Meade had anticipated. Longstreet strongly opposed the plan, believing that an attack on such a defensible position was suicidal, but again Lee refused to be swayed.

On the morning of 3 July Ewell attempted to atone for his previous lack of initiative, attacking Slocum's Corps at Culp's Hill and in the Baltimore Pike area. For more than three hours the Confederate forces endured a punishing artillery barrage and rifle fire in their efforts to capture the positions. After taking heavy losses in their numerous attempts to breach the defenses, Ewell's troops were forced to withdraw to their previous positions. Two hours later at 1300 hours the Confederate artillery along the two-mile front began a bombardment of the Union center. An artillery duel followed, which lasted more than two hours. Then the Union artillery withdrew to conserve ammunition and await the anticipated Confederate attack. With the silence of the guns Longstreet unwillingly ordered the advance of Major General George E Pickett's 15,000 men. Pickett's troops closed the gap between themselves and the defenders and the Confederate artillery ceased fire in deference to its own troops. The Union forces then opened fire with rifle and cannon. Within minutes more than 9000 Confederate troops lay dead or wounded and only several hundred ever reached the Union lines. Although bravely executed 'Pickett's Charge' was a complete disaster. As the survivors re-

turned to their own lines it was evident that, at least for the time being, the spirit of the Army of Northern Virginia was crushed.

The final attack of the day was an assault on the right flank of the Confederate position by Brigadier General EJ Farnsworth's cavalry. The attack was successfully repulsed by the Confederates and Farnsworth himself was killed. In the late afternoon Jeb Stuart finally pinpointed Lee's position after searching the Pennsylvanian countryside for more than one week. He attempted to reach Gettysburg, but was intercepted by Union forces commanded by Brigadier General George Armstrong Custer several miles from the town. After a heated skirmish, Stuart was able to break off the engagement to continue his search for the Army of Northern Virginia.

Although Lee reconsolidated his army on Seminary Ridge to await a Union counterattack, the battlefield remained quiet throughout the morning of 4 July. By afternoon a severe storm struck, making further action virtually impossible. That evening Lee began to withdraw from the area. Although Meade realized that Lee was in retreat, he did not pursue the Confederate army until 7 July and that pursuit by Sedgwick's Corps was apparently a token effort only. On 13 July Lee successfully crossed the Potomac River without incident. Meade was criticized for his failure to launch a strong counterattack against Lee's retreating forces, but the Army of the Potomac had lost approximately 20 percent of its strength and Lee had lost nearly 30 percent of his army, for a combined total of more than 50,000 men killed, wounded, missing or captured. Just as Lee had no recourse but to retreat, Meade's only logical option was to pause and

Left: Union forces attempted to bypass the Confederate fortress at Vicksburg by cutting a canal through a spit of land opposite.
Below: the besiegers of Vicksburg included Sherman's corps and some of its positions are illustrated in this sketch.

recoup his army's strength before launching it into another battle. The Battle of Gettysburg would have far-reaching consequences for the Confederate cause, perhaps most importantly in the loss of irreplaceable manpower.

While Lee's invasion of the North was being planned and executed, a major campaign was being staged in the West. Grant was once again concentrating his efforts on the division of the South through the capture of Vicksburg and control of the Mississippi River Basin. From January through March several methods were employed by Grant's Army of the Tennessee to capture Vicksburg. Sherman's XV Corps attempted to bypass Vicksburg by cutting a canal across the narrow finger of land opposite the city but this failed when spring floods inundated the area. Another attempt to navigate the Yazoo River tributaries and capture Yazoo City was thwarted by persistent Confederate harassment. Finally Grant adopted a new strategy which would circumvent the hazardous, easily-defensible northern approaches to Vicksburg to attack the city from the south. In late March Major General John A McClernand and Major General James B McPherson's corps began to march south along the west bank of the Mississippi. Sherman's corps remained in position north of Vicksburg to help disguise Grant's intentions.

On 6 April Admiral David Porter, who was again involved with Grant's operations, began moving his flotilla south, running the gauntlet of the Vicksburg artillery with gunboats and cargo steamers. As the Union corps marched, they captured first New Carthage and then Bruinsburg, Louisiana. On 30 April Grant began ferrying his troops across the river into Mississippi. This surprised the Confederate command, which spent several days pondering Grant's possible objectives. Those days gave Grant the time he needed to steal the initiative from the Confederates permanently. On 1 May Grant defeated an outnumbered Confederate contingent at Port Gibson and again astonished them by moving east toward Jackson, Mississippi, rather than north toward Vicksburg. By 7 May Sherman was on the move to join Grant's main army.

As Grant marched toward the state capital, General JE Johnston (overall commander of the region) arrived in the city. For the moment his army was small, but he expected reinforcements from the East which would swell his force to 30,000 men. General John C Pemberton commanded approximately 30,000 troops in the Vicksburg garrison. Their combined forces would have been a match for Grant's 51,000 troops. What Johnston did not realize was that Pemberton had left almost 10,000 troops in Vicksburg, and had scattered the remainder of his men over a 20-mile front. Pemberton, under orders from Jefferson Davis, had left this defensive force behind and had then attempted to sever Grant's lines

of supply and communication. However, there were no such lines. From his campaign against Vicksburg in 1862 Grant had learned that his army could live off the land in the region around the Mississippi River. By the time Pemberton realized his mistake, Grant had taken Raymond, Mississippi. On 14 May the Union army captured Jackson, Mississippi, destroyed its railhead and captured a large quantity of supplies. Grant then reversed the direction of his army and on 16 May defeated Pemberton's forces in a bitter confrontation at Champion's Hill. After that defeat Pemberton made another grave miscalculation. Instead of moving his army northeast to link with Johnston, he left more than 1700 men and accompanying artillery batteries as a rear guard and retreated to Vicksburg. Those men and 18 cannon were captured on 17 May at the Big Black River by Grant's advancing troops and Pemberton was now trapped and isolated.

By 19 May Grant had reached Vicksburg and he launched two consecutive attacks immediately. Both attacks failed, primarily because of the strength of the garrison defenses and the staunch resistance of the fresh troops who had remained in the city during Pemberton's march. Grant was anxious to take the city quickly, aware that Johnston was to his rear, and on 21 May he bombarded it in preparation for a third assault. Grant had positioned McClernand's XIII Corps southeast of Vicksburg, McPherson's XVII Corps to the east, and Sherman's XV Corps on the northern flank. When the attack was launched only McClernand's forces made any significant gains, but without reinforcements they were forced to withdraw. Although the Vicksburg campaign had been extremely successful in destroying Confederate rail lines, capturing supplies and equipment and disrupting Confederate operations in the entire area, Grant was disgruntled by his army's inability to take the city and decided to lay siege to Vicksburg. His decision was also influenced by the intelligence that Johnston's reinforcements had been diverted to join Lee's invasion of the North, reducing the threat to him considerably.

Grant's main concern was to conduct an effective siege. He appointed Captains F E Prime and Cyrus B Comstock to conduct the preparations, giving his engineers full rein to implement the operation. Throughout May and June the battle of Vicksburg became one of trench warfare. By day the two forces assaulted, fired at and mined the opposing trenches and by night they rebuilt and repaired the damages. By the end of June the Union forces had dug several miles of trenches around Vicksburg and Grant's army had grown to 70,000 men. A siege of this magnitude was virtually unprecedented and, while curious civilians roamed the Union trenches bringing food and drink and promoting a carnival atmosphere, the defenders within the city were rapidly depleting their supplies. Finally Pemberton was forced to admit that he had no recourse but to surrender.

On the morning of 3 July Pemberton sent an envoy to Grant's headquarters submitting his terms for surrender. Grant's demand for immediate and unconditional surrender insulted and infuriated the Confederate commander yet he had no alternative but to comply. On the morning of 4 July Grant accepted the long-awaited formal surrender of Vicksburg. The entire Confederate army could be classified lost, being either killed or captured, and Grant acquired the garrison artillery and more than 60,000 small arms. Five days later Port Hudson fell to Union forces, placing the entire Mississippi River under Union control. Grant had successfully captured Vicksburg by applying the concept of total war. He had campaigned throughout the entire area, destroying the ability of the Confederate forces to wage war. He then set about destroying their will, using every conceivable method – some of which were considered too extreme by those who believed in the 'gentlemanly art' of warfare.

With Meade's victory at Gettysburg and Grant's successful operations to bisect the Confederacy along the Mississippi River, the Union planned to divide the Confederacy again by moving forces from the Mississippi River to the Atlantic Coast. A large segment of Grant's army struck east toward Tennessee, particularly the area around Chattanooga. Its route was across the manufacturing heartland of the South, and it was to destroy those centers and the vital east-west rail lines. The fall of the Mississippi, attacks against key objectives on the Atlantic coast and the blockade of the Confederate coastlines made the isolation of the primary Confederate states an imminent possibility. If successful the final phase of the Union strategy would prove fatal to the Southern war effort.

Lincoln strongly favored the invasion of Tennessee. General AE Burnside had spent several months training his newly formed Army of the Ohio and in mid-August 1863 he captured Knoxville and the Cumberland Gap in rapid succession. The Union had unopposed control of western Tennessee. Confederate forces in the area consolidated to make their stance around Chattanooga. To complement Burnside's activities General William Rosecrans' Army of the Cumberland moved across the Tennessee River toward Chattanooga. Rather than directly confront the Confederate army he decided to surround Chattanooga and force the Confederates to attack him in an effort to break his stranglehold on the city. General Braxton Bragg, commander of the Army of Tennessee at Chattanooga, realized Rosecrans' intentions and maneuvered his army south of the city into Georgia. Rosecrans mistook that move for retreat and divided his army into three corps, sending each by a separate route to pursue Bragg. Rosecrans had spread his army over so wide an area that each corps was isolated from the other two. Bragg, whose army's numbers had increased since he fought Rosecrans at Murfreesboro, decided to take the initiative. Believing that Rosecrans had divided his army into only two columns, Bragg chose to attack what was actually the center corps of the Army of the Cumberland's three-pronged advance. The discord between Bragg and his officers precluded any such attack, but the time wasted by the Army of Tennessee permitted Rosecrans to correct the overextension of his army.

Timing was a crucial factor. As Rosecrans reconsolidated his army Bragg awaited reinforcements in the form of Longstreet's Corps from the Army of Northern Virginia. These troops were travelling through the Carolinas and Georgia, because the more direct rail route through Knoxville had been severed by Burnside's forces. On the morning of 18 September, with the leading brigades of Longstreet's Corps arriving, Bragg initiated an attack on the Union left flank, which required the Confederate troops to cross Chickamauga Creek. This plan was thwarted when it was discovered that Union defenders controlled the bridges and primary fording sites. Throughout the day Confederate forces struggled to cross the creek and it was only under cover of darkness that they were able to accomplish their task. General Rosecrans reacted by sending reinforcements to that flank. As the fighting was renewed on the morning of 19 September both armies were surprised by the number of enemy troops that they encountered. The front line of the battlefield ranged over six miles of densely wooded terrain and repeated attacks and counterattacks produced no clear advantage. By late evening Longstreet and two more of his brigades arrived on the scene. After a fruitless and often dangerous search for Bragg, he withdrew to a safe distance and awaited Bragg's messenger.

On the morning of 20 September, with his army fully complemented, Bragg decided to divide his force. He sent half under the command of General Polk to renew the attack on the Union flank, while the other half commanded by Longstreet waited in reserve to exploit any advantage gained by Union attempts to protect its left flank. During the night Rosecrans had reorganized his forces at a more defensible position and had reinforced the exact target area of Polk's attack. Consequently, although the Confederates made repeated attempts to breach the defenses, they were repulsed and forced to withdrawn. Longstreet then noticed a large gap in the Union lines where a division had been removed to join the left flank defenses. Longstreet launched his attack and the Union right flank crumbled. He then swung to his right and began to sweep toward the Union rear. The Confederate advance was brought to a halt at a ridge near Snodgrass House, when the First Division arrived to bolster the Union troops. Longstreet immediately sent word to Bragg stating

Above: the Battle of Lookout Mountain was fought in mist.

that he could overcome the Union resistance with the aid of reinforcements. The problem that had plagued the Army of the Tennessee and created discord among its officer ranks surfaced. Bragg had persistently refused to listen to the advice or opinions of his subordinates and again he would not alter his battle scheme, or draw from Polk's forces to aid Longstreet. This intransigence allowed the Union army to escape destruction. Rosecrans and a small portion of his army had retreated after Longstreet's initial attack. Major General George H Thomas' forces remained and he reorganized them with the remnants of the other corps which remained on the field. They continued to fight, withdrawing slowly toward Chattanooga until Thomas reached a defensible position and halted his troops. There he awaited a Confederate attack which never materialized.

Bragg considered possession of the battlefield tantamount to victory and did not pursue his strong advantage. The Battle of Chickamauga ended with nearly 18,000 Confederate and more than 16,000 Union casualties. Although the Army of Tennessee held the field and had captured some 50 artillery pieces and several thousand infantry weapons, Bragg had settled for a minor victory when he might have destroyed the Army of the Cumberland. General Thomas' exceptional defensive maneuvers and staunch resistance enabled his army to march in good order from its final defensive position to Chattanooga, and earned him the title 'Rock of Chickamauga.'

The Army of the Cumberland moved into Chattanooga and Bragg initiated plans for a siege of the city. Chattanooga lies on the Tennessee River and is surrounded by mountains through which there were few access roads. As Bragg positioned the bulk of his army south of the city, he reasoned that the only avenue of resupply for the Union army would be the river. He sent part of his army southwest to Lookout Mountain where they would command the river at Moccasin Bend. The largest portion of his army was sent southeast of the city to Missionary Ridge. Bragg's tactics failed to take account of several crucial factors necessary to the execution of a successful siege. First he failed to maneuver troops north of the Tennessee River to complete the encirclement of the city. He also ignored the fact that the successful conclusion of the Union Vicksburg campaign meant the release of a large number of troops who could be directed toward any disputed area in the West. Nor did Bragg take into consideration the influence of other events in the war effort, primarily in the East where Lee might at any time require Longstreet's Corps. Finally Bragg refused to acknowledge the depth of the resentment of his officer corps or the influence their dissent had on the performance of his army. Jefferson Davis was aware of the situation and appeared at Chattanooga to reconcile the difference between the commander and his officers. Bragg and Davis were long time friends and Davis would not take action against him. Davis had no objective view of the officers' position and let matters stand, confident that the officers would not allow their personal feelings to influence their military obligations. He would be proved wrong.

The Union command was not idle while the Army of Tennessee was being deployed around Chattanooga. Hooker was marching from Virginia with troops from the XI and XII Corps of the Army of the Potomac and from the West Sherman was leading the Army of the Tennessee to Chattanooga. Bragg had sent a cavalry expedition to harass the Union lines of supply and communication around the city, but it was a minimal effort which did little to slow the approach of reinforcements.

On 23 October Grant arrived at Chattanooga. Only a few days earlier he had become commander of all Union armies in the West. One of his first decisions had been to replace Rosecrans with General George H Thomas. Thomas submitted a plan to Grant which would open new avenues of supply north of the city across the Tennessee River and Raccoon Mountain. Grant accepted Thomas' plan and Hooker's forces, which were approaching northwest of the city, were sent to Brown's Ferry to secure the area and protect the pontoon bridges which were erected. Within days the resupply problem was solved and the Union forces had only to await Sherman's arrival before initiating their next phase. Bragg's reaction to the reopening of Union supply lines was to send Longstreet east to besiege Burnside's forces at Knoxville. Except perhaps as a weak diversionary tactic to draw Union troops to that location, Bragg's action was futile and displayed excessively poor judgment.

Sherman's army arrived at Chattanooga in mid-November and it was decided that Sherman would take charge of the main attack against Missionary Ridge. Initiating the assault involved an intricate maneuver during which Sherman would march his army from the Raccoon Mountain range, cross Hooker's pontoon bridge, swing north, recross the Tennessee River and finally launch his attack on Bragg's far right flank. The maneuver was intended to be completed for an attack on 21 November, but a severe storm damaged the pontoon bridge and Sherman was forced to leave one division behind and delay the completion of his march by three days. The addition of that division to Hooker's force caused Grant to reevaluate the situation and schedule an assault on Lookout Mountain. On 23 November Grant received information that Bragg was removing his army from the field and to test that fact Grant ordered an assault on the center of Missionary Ridge at a point known as Orchard Knob. Confederate resistance was staunch, indicating to Grant that Bragg was not withdrawing. After a bitter confrontation Union superior numbers overwhelmed the Confederate outpost. The following day Hooker's troops attacked Lookout Mountain. With a six to one Union superiority it was obvious that, despite their advantageous position, the Confederate troops could not possibly withstand the pressure. They made a final desperate attempt to hold the Union advance at Craven's House, but after heavy casualties they abandoned their position and returned to the main body of the army under cover of darkness. 'The Battle Above the Clouds' was ended and Hooker's troops occupied an excellent position for the ensuing battle. As Hooker assaulted Lookout Mountain, Sherman completed his maneuver and launched his own attack. Unfortunately he mistook Battery Heights for the northern edge of Missionary Ridge and, although he captured it, he betrayed his presence to the Confederate army.

On the morning of 25 November Sherman launched six divisions against the lone Confederate division of General Patrick Cleburne. The fierce melee which followed the attack continued for many hours and, although the Union troops repeatedly attempted to reach the top of the ridge and overwhelm Cleburne, they were finally forced to withdraw. As Sherman's assault crumbled, Grant impatiently awaited Hooker's attack on the Confederate left flank. Finally unable to risk the effect of further delay, Grant ordered Thomas' army to make a frontal assault on Missionary Ridge. It was a dangerous tactic, but as Thomas' forces advanced it soon became apparent that there was a sharp decrease in Confederate fire being directed against them. It was then realized that Bragg was in full retreat. The Union army was amazed that Bragg had relinquished such a strong position. Evidently the Confederate troops, knowing the Union forces to be on both flanks, could not accept the sight of a Union army massing for a frontal assault. The attitude of the Confederate officers gave the troops little incentive to stand and fight.

Although Grant ordered a pursuit of the Army of the Tennessee, Cleburne's division provided an aggressive rearguard for the Confederate army. Grant's 60,000 troops suffered approximately 10 percent casualties, but almost 7000 of Bragg's 37,000 men were lost. The missing numbered 4000, but it was clear that these men had simply decided to take a short respite from the army. Grant advanced to Knoxville, and Longstreet made a final unsuccessful bid to capture the city before Grant arrived. After his failure Longstreet withdrew to winter quarters in North Carolina.

Grant had broken the siege at Chattanooga and had secured the state of Tennessee for the Union. Jefferson Davis was forced to remove Bragg from command, and replaced him with General JE Johnston. As 1863 drew to a close the Confederacy was faced with the prospect of fighting a strictly defensive war. Unable to launch another invasion of the North, the Confederate states could only hope to prolong the war successfully until the North grew weary and an honorable peace could be made.

4 SURRENDER AT APPOMATTOX

Above: Lieutenant General Ulysses Grant assumed command of all the Union armies in March 1864.
Left: Grant appointed William Sherman to command the Union armies in the west.

The early months of 1864 differed from the same time period of the previous years in that there was a decided advantage for one of the participants. The Union success in the East and West produced a confidence that the North would soon achieve victory. Optimistic Northerners predicted that the South would be defeated by summer. One important figure in the Union command thought otherwise. General Grant, who was made General-in-Chief of all Union armies in March 1864, realized that although weakened the Confederates' will to fight remained strong. Grant anticipated at least one and perhaps two more years of war.

Upon the assumption of his new rank Grant made several changes in the military command structure. He placed his former commander General Halleck, described as a 'first rate clerk,' in a staff position in Washington to act as a liaison officer between the military and the government. He promoted Sherman to command all Union armies in the West and placed Major General James McPherson in command of the Army of the Tennessee. He also transferred many rear echelon officers to combat positions. Major General Phillip H Sheridan, recognized for his contributions in the West, was given command of the cavalry of the Army of the Potomac. As the changes were being carried out, Grant joined the Army of the Potomac. Although General Meade remained the acting commander, Grant considered that his own presence there facing Lee was of utmost importance. Grant had only two months to complete his reorganization programs and formulate a new strategy

before spring would again bring the opposing armies together. Grant's main strategy was two-fold. Sherman was to lead his armies in an approach from the West to Atlanta and the coast. His path would traverse the industrial heartland of the South, eliminating Southern manufacturing capacity and bisecting the Confederacy once again. Grant with the Army of the Potomac would continue to oppose the Army of Northern Virginia with the goal of capturing Richmond.

By the first week of May, Grant was prepared to launch his spring campaign in the East. He hoped to maneuver Lee into a position where the Army of the Potomac could destroy the Confederate army, but realized that a campaign of attrition was far more likely. On 4 May Grant ordered General Franz Sigel's forces to advance in the Shenandoah Valley and General Benjamin Butler's Army of the James toward Richmond south of the James River. The Army of the Potomac crossed the Rapidan River at Germanna Ford on a course similar to that taken by the Union army prior to the Battle of Chancellorsville.

Lee watched the movement of the Army of the Potomac with interest. He was being presented with an opportunity to attack Grant's army on its right flank as the Union army marched, yet Lee was hesitant to do so. Much of Lee's earlier success can be attributed to his accurate assessment of his adversaries' characters, but Grant was an unknown

quantity. The opportunity to attack the Union army on its flank could not be ignored. On 5 May near the Wilderness Tavern and the site of Jackson's famous attack against Hooker, Lee attacked the Army of the Potomac. That assault lacked coordination and as troops arrived on both sides the first day of the Battle of the Wilderness raged fiercely along a five-mile front but produced no strong advantage for either army. The following day Hancock's II Corps attacked AP Hill's Corps on the Confederate right flank and appeared to be succeeding until Longstreet's Corps arrived and entered the fray. There was a great deal of confusion as Longstreet ordered a counterattack. In that attempt Longstreet was seriously wounded by a volley from his own troops on virtually the same site where Jackson had been mortally wounded the year before. Lee rushed forward, halting the counterattack and ordering the corps to stand and reorganize.

Hancock had been driven back and for five hours the Confederates regrouped in preparation for an assault. At approximately 1600 hours the Confederate forces launched their attack. Hancock's men had prepared defensive breastworks, but the Confederate troops overwhelmed that position. Victory seemed imminent but a brush fire broke out which forced the Confederate troops to halt. When the fire subsided Grant ordered a counterattack and recaptured the breastworks. With that action the Battle of the Wilderness ended and both armies halted to reconsolidate. It had been a particularly gruesome battle, as many of the casualties were incurred during the fire that raced through the undergrowth. Grant listed 1700 casualties from his 100,000 troops, while Lee's losses numbered approximately 8000 of his 60,000-man army.

In the aftermath of the battle Lee watched for Grant's next move. He was surprised when on 7 May, after a brief though heated skirmish between Jeb

Stuart's cavalry and Union troops north of Spotsylvania, it was reported that Grant had immediately continued his march south. It had become a pattern for Union generals to act slowly after a major battle, usually withdrawing to a safe distance, yet Grant seemed determined to continue on his course. Lee was at a decided disadvantage. The south's officer corps was seriously depleted by the losses which had been sustained over the past months. Along with Longstreet, Hill was also incapacitated with a serious illness, but Lee had no time to wait for them to recover. He had to react quickly to Grant's latest maneuver.

Lee promoted Richard H Anderson to command Longstreet's Corps and ordered him to set out for Spotsylvania no later than 0300 hours on 8 May. Anderson quickly took control of the corps and started the march at 2300 hours on 7 May. Anderson's precipitate action would prove to be the saving factor for the Army of Northern Virginia in the impending engagement. In the predawn hours of 8 May Stuart's cavalry was engaged with Sheridan's cavalry and lead elements of Grant's army as they too advanced on Spotsylvania. Stuart realized that if Grant took the crossroads at Spotsylvania the Army of the Potomac would hold a strong position between the Army of Northern Virginia and Richmond. Stuart sent a message requesting reinforcements, which reached Anderson as his troops halted to prepare their break-

fast. Anderson reacted immediately and by 0800 hours Brigadier General JB Kershaw's division arrived to relieve the beleaguered Confederate cavalry. The infantry successfully halted the Union advance and Sheridan withdrew temporarily to assess the situation. After tentatively testing the Confederate strength at several points along the line with the aid of General GK Warren's corps, Sheridan was forced merely to harass the Confederates while he awaited Grant's arrival. If Anderson had not begun his march when he did, Stuart's cavalry would certainly have been overwhelmed and the Army of Northern Virginia placed in grave peril.

As Anderson's full corps arrived they began building fortified trenches to strengthen their defenses. When Meade and Grant finally arrived on the scene on 9 May, they were amazed to see that in 24 hours the Confederate forces had constructed fortifications which usually took 72 hours. It was obvious that Grant would have to launch a major effort to take the Confederate position. Spotsylvania had developed into exactly the type of battle Grant wanted to avoid. Grant began by ordering Sheridan's cavalry to circle and harass Lee's rear area. After a brief respite for the Confederate cavalry, Lee sent Stuart to counter Sheridan. That activity would continue until 11 May when just north of Richmond at Yellow Tavern the opposing cavalry met and Jeb Stuart was killed. His death was another serious blow to the Confederacy.

As Grant sent troops forward to assess the strength of various points along the Confederate defense the Army of Northern Virginia continued to arrive. By the evening of 9 May they were in position but in the hasty attempts to bolster the defenders a salient dubbed the 'Mule Shoe' developed in the Confederate line. The salient caused a great deal of anxiety in the Confederate command, but General Ewell was convinced that if adequately supported by artillery the defenses could withstand a Union assault. Ewell also pointed out that the salient would obviously be the primary Union target and that the Confederate army could direct all its attention to protecting that area. His assessment was correct and on 10 May Grant launched numerous assaults at various points along the perimeter of the salient without notable success. Brigadier General Upton's brigade managed to make a slight gain but was swiftly driven back by a Confederate counterattack. However that particular location drew Grant's attention and it was there that he decided to concentrate his main attack.

On 11 May 75 percent of the Union army was maneuvering around the salient, but Lee did not recognize that the lack of Union success on the previous day had not altered Grant's determination. Lee misinterpreted the Union maneuvers as the prelude to withdrawal and therefore ordered his army to make ready to march and he also withdrew the artillery which had protected the salient to a position for rapid deployment elsewhere. At 0840 hours on 12 May Grant ordered an artillery barrage and then sent Hancock's Corps formed in a grand column against the Mule Shoe. The Union forces overwhelmed General Edward Johnson's Division at odds of ten to one and then carried through to the line of General John Gordon's troops. In spite of the initial success, Hancock's troops floundered, disorganized by the momentum of their charge. In the brief pause General Gordon organized his own and General Robert Rodes' divisions into a second line of defense. As the melee continued both Lee and Grant sent reinforcements to the western sector of the salient. The battle there, known as the Bloody Angle, raged for more than six hours with neither army able to force the other to withdraw. In fact the two armies remained locked in repeated attacks until 18 May. Finally exhausted, the Union army pulled away from the engagement. A combined total of more than 10,000 casualties had been sustained in an area of approximately one square mile, making the battlefield at Spotsylvania one of the bloodiest sites of the Civil War.

Grant set out almost immediately to continue on his course toward Richmond. The attrition of the campaign was beginning to tell. Although Grant had ample reserves on which to draw, Lee's army was rapidly diminishing, for instance, Ewell's corps had been reduced to little more than division strength. The only possible hope for the Army of Northern Virginia was to position itself carefully where it could best fight defensive battles geared to protect Richmond. Grant continued to travel south toward the capital, probing Lee's army for opportunities to catch the Confederates in a weak position. The armies clashed first at North Anna on 23 May and again at Totopotomy on 30 May. On 3 June Grant launched a massive frontal attack against Lee near Mechanicsville, Virginia, at the Battle of Cold Harbor. Fierce fighting continued there until 12 June and, although both army sustained many casualties, Grant could not dislodge the defenders.

The costly battle drained the strength of Lee's army, but after Cold Harbor he succeeded in maneuvering the Army of Northern Virginia to a strong defensive position around Richmond. Grant immediately realized that any attempt to capture or besiege Richmond would be futile so long as Petersburg continued to function as a primary resupply source. In mid-June Grant set out to capture Petersburg and thereby isolate Richmond. Once Petersburg fell, and Grant was certain it would fall, Lee would be forced to either surrender or take the offensive against the numerically-superior Union forces.

The defense of Petersburg had been in the hands of General PGT Beauregard for some time and, although the defensive capabilities of the city appeared to be more than sufficient, in actual fact they were sadly lacking. The city was surrounded by more than 10 miles of trenchworks, including 55 redoubts and fortifications called the Dimmock Line. It was a strong defensive barrier. The problem was that Beauregard's garrison troops numbered less than 3000 men, the majority of whom were either too old or too young for regular service, or had been previously wounded and were unable to rejoin their field units. When Beauregard's men were in position along the Dimmock Line, there were sections where enemy troops could advance undetected until they were well within the outer perimeter of the city. Too few men attempting to cover the defenses which stretched over rolling hills caused a precarious situation for the Confederate army.

On 9 June while the Army of the Potomac was still at Cold Harbor, Grant ordered Major General Butler's Army of the James to attack Petersburg. In the engagement dubbed 'The Battle of Patients and Penitents' Butler's forces made a poor showing, believing the Confederate garrison defenses to be much stronger than they actually were. The cavalry division which had accompanied Butler's army discovered areas of weakness and their commander reported those positions to Grant. By 15 June the Army of the Potomac was arriving at Petersburg. Grant's position opposite Lee at Cold Harbor had been abandoned and during the march to Petersburg

Below: Petersburg, Virginia, was the railhead for the Army of Northern Virginia.

Right: Grant began his attack on Petersburg in June 1864 with an all-out assault.

Below: Petersburg, Virginia, was the railhead for the Army of Northern Virginia.

Grant's engineers accomplished one of the greatest engineering feats in military history. Between 1600 and 2400 hours on 14 June they constructed a 2100ft-long pontoon bridge across the James River over which the bulk of the Army of the Potomac marched.

At 0700 hours the same day Major General William F Smith's XVIII Corps, which had crossed the river earlier, was assembled for an attack on Petersburg. Rather than initiate the assault, Smith decided to reconnoiter the area. During the delay Beauregard sent an urgent message to Lee requesting immediate reinforcements. Finally nine hours later Smith was prepared to launch his attack. His entire corps had arrived and was assembled to advance as soon as the Union artillery barrage began. The corps waited but no cannon were fired. Smith realized that the artillery officer had not been informed of the attack. It was 1900 hours before the artillery could be brought into action, but when the ill-managed attack began the Confederate forces were immediately overwhelmed.

The combination of artillery and infantry opened a one-mile gap in the Confederate defensive line, but Smith did not pursue his advantage. The ease with which his men had overrun the defenses led Smith to believe that Beauregard was attempting to draw the Union troops into a trap. Smith halted the attack and ordered his corps to prepare their own defenses when he might well have taken the city that evening.

While Smith's corps prepared their defenses, Hancock's Corps which had been ferried across the James River on the morning of 14 June, arrived. Hancock had spent the entire day marching and countermarching in search of nonexistent reference and assembly points specified in his orders. On reaching Petersburg and being informed that he was to have participated in the battle, Hancock lost his temper and ordered his troops to bivouac. He and his men had been without food or rest and Hancock himself was suffering from his unhealed Gettysburg wound. He was in no frame of mind to order his

troops to advance over unfamiliar terrain. By the early hours of 16 June Burnside's IX Corps had arrived and Beauregard had received 5000 additional troops. At 1800 hours, with support from Burnside, Hancock attacked the reinforced Confederate positions. The attack was decisively repulsed. The same day also brought Grant and Meade to the battlefield and when Lee was informed of this he immediately realized the seriousness of the situation and began an earnest attempt at reinforcement. Anderson's Division was among the first to arrive from Richmond and they were almost immediately engaged by Butler's army. Anderson succeeded in repulsing Butler's attack and the following morning Pickett's Division renewed the assault, removing any chance Butler might have had of blocking the influx of reinforcements and isolating Beauregard from Lee.

On the morning of 17 July Beauregard had more than 14,000 men against a Union force of some 80,000. Meade reviewed the situation and decided to concentrate his efforts on the Confederate positions which guarded the primary road into Petersburg. If the two hills which the Confederates occupied could be taken the city would become easier prey. The hills were quickly captured in surprise attacks, but Burnside's support failed to arrive. Burnside sent a messenger to Brigadier General James Ledlie, commander of the support troops, and when he was found still asleep, he denied knowledge of any orders to prepare for an advance. Another division was called upon to reinforce Burnside but the momentum had been lost and the Confederates reorganized to repulse the attack. Hancock, whose wound was so inflamed that he could no longer command, put General David Birney in charge of the assault on the Confederate hill. The Union troops captured the position, but without further orders or insight into the overall objective Birney halted on the hill to reorganize his forces.

The Confederate defenses were in chaos and Beauregard sent Lee an urgent message requesting that the Army of Northern Virginia march to Petersburg. In the Union camp Meade was furious, castigating his officers for failing to pursue their advantage. He issued orders for the army to charge en masse, giving his officers full rein to exploit any advantage they achieved. On the morning of 18 June the Army of the Potomac attacked, only to find the Confederate outer defenses deserted. This caught Meade off guard and he lost several hours issuing new orders. It was noon before the advance was renewed and by that time Lee and his army had arrived to defend the city. Although Union forces launched numerous assaults, none was successful and as the casualty rates climbed Grant halted further action.

Grant then spent several days reorganizing the army, after which he attacked the Jerusalem Plank Road in an effort to outflank Lee. This maneuver was repulsed by AP Hill's corps and Grant was forced to admit that he had completely lost the initiative. In less than one week his army had suffered 12,000 casualties and the public outcry over losses coupled with the impending presidential elections gave Grant

abilities by leading the assault, politics intervened. Grant was reminded by members of his staff of the social and political repercussions if Ferrero's forces should suffer heavy casualties, as it might be implied that Grant sacrificed black rather than white soldiers. Despite pleas from Ferrero and his men, Grant changed the orders and Burnside maneuvered Ledlie's corps to spearhead the assault.

At 1530 hours on 30 July the troops were prepared for the assault and the fuse to the underground explosives was lit. After waiting for almost an hour for the explosion two men entered the tunnel and relit the fuse. At 1645 hours the 8000 pounds of explosives ripped a 60ft-wide, 170ft-long crater in the Confederate defenses. The fortification atop the blast site was obliterated and for almost 150 yards on each side of the crater Confederate troops abandoned their positions in terror. Ledlie's Division advanced into the crater, from which the battle takes its name, but did not continue forward. Other divisions advanced but each followed Ledlie's example, crowding into the crater. The Confederates were incapable of resistance, but the Union commanders refused to pursue their advantage. After more than two hours Burnside committed his reserves, Ferrero's Division, which charged through the crater. The effort disorganized the black units and their piecemeal attack on the recovered Confederate defenders failed. Lee ordered artillery to fire on the Crater and finally after taking nearly 4500 casualties Grant withdrew his forces, calling it the 'saddest affair' he had ever witnessed. Burnside bore the brunt of the blame for the failure of the assault and was later court-martialed.

From that time until March 1865 the battle around Petersburg and Richmond became one of trench warfare with repeated Union attempts to test the Confederate defenses and restrict the flow of supplies to the cities. There was a brief renewal of activity involving segments of Grant's and Lee's armies in the early fall. When Grant began his march toward Petersburg he had replaced General Sigel in the Shenandoah Valley with General David Hunter. As Hunter began to take control of the Valley, Lee sent Early's corps and two divisions of cavalry commanded by General Wade Hampton to counter the Union threat. After defeating Hunter near Lynchburg, Early decided that he could best aid Lee by drawing Grant's attention away from Richmond and to accomplish that task Early moved his corps to threaten Washington. By 11 July 1864 Early was within five miles of the White House and the people of the capital were in panic. On 12 July Early's Corps skirmished with Union forces at Fort Stevens, but in the face of increasing Union reinforcements Early withdrew to carry out operations in northern Virginia. When Washington was threatened Grant sent Sheridan's cavalry to deal with Early. After more than one month away from the Army of the Potomac, Sheridan

no option but to cease the unproductive attacks and lay siege to Petersburg. Throughout June and most of July the Union forces entrenched themselves and although minor skirmishing occurred the stalemate continued. At the end of July troops of Lieutenant Colonel Henry Pleasant's 48th Pennsylvania Veteran Volunteers Regiment of Burnside's corps hit upon the idea of tunnelling under the Confederate lines of defense to plant an explosive charge under one of the fortifications. Although the idea sounded absurd to other regiments and officers, the majority of soldiers in the 48th Regiment were coal miners from Pennsylvania with the knowledge and skill to accomplish such a task. The idea was finally explained to General Grant and his approval received.

On 30 July 1864 the 500ft-long tunnel was completed and the explosives emplaced. Several days before Hancock and Sherman had created a diversion at Richmond, drawing all but three Confederate divisions away from the Petersburg defenses. Orders had been given for a major assault on the Confederate position after the detonation, led by Brigadier General Edward Ferrero's Negro Division, the freshest troops of Burnside's corps. Although the black troops had conducted themselves well in various incidents and were eager to demonstrate their encountered and defeated Early at Obequon Creek, near Winchester, on 19 September. Three days later he again successfully engaged Early at Fisher's Hill. Confident that Early was no longer a threat Sheridan maneuvered to sever Lee's main supply routes, but Early was not so easily discouraged and on 19 October he attacked Sheridan's forces at Cedar Creek, Virginia. Sheridan was not with his troops at the time and the surprise of the Confederate attack routed the Union forces. Early then paused to allow his troops to forage for food before pursuing his enemy. That halt proved fatal, as it gave Sheridan time to reach his men and rally them. When Sheridan counterattacked, Early's Corps was virtually destroyed, giving Sheridan and the Union indisputable control of the Shenandoah Valley.

During the same months that Grant's Eastern Campaign toward Richmond and Petersburg was in progress, Sherman was pursuing the objectives Grant had established in the broad war strategy. From Chattanooga Sherman set out toward Atlanta with the combined forces of Major General Thomas' Army of the Cumberland, Major General John Schofield's Army of the Ohio and Major General McPherson's Army of the Tennessee. Together the armies totalled more than 100,000 men. Opposing Sherman was Bragg's Army of Tennessee, its strength and effectiveness seriously eroded by a deterioration in morale and unprecedented numbers of desertions. Finally Jefferson Davis was forced to remove Bragg, hiding the truth of Bragg's ineptitude by creating the role of Special Military Advisor to the President for him. When General Joseph E Johnston assumed command of the Army of Tennessee he discovered the extent of the disintegration of the army. He began his reorganization by offering an amnesty to deserters who returned voluntarily. He initiated an extensive furlough system during the early months of 1864, designed not only to refresh the troops but also to alleviate the burden of their maintenance on the army. Johnston also introduced rigid drill instructions geared to the type of defensive fighting that he knew the army would have to employ in the months ahead.

By the spring of 1864 the morale and confidence of the Army of Tennessee had been restored, but Davis was not satisfied. He resented Johnston's successful revitalization of the army and harassed Johnston with orders to initiate an offensive. Yet Johnston quietly ignored Davis' interference and continued his defensive strategy, confident that he could cause havoc to the Union armies' advance. One offensive tactic Johnston did employ involved sending General Nathan Forrest's cavalry to conduct raids in Kentucky, Tennessee and the Mississippi River area. Throughout March he retained points in Kentucky as far north as Paduca. During the summer he continued to roam the assigned regions, capturing the Union headquarters in Memphis in late August. He was constantly pursued but was never defeated. In early fall he withdrew to rejoin the army.

In the first week of May Sherman moved his army into Georgia. The army was brought to a halt at a plateau near Dalton where Confederate forces held a ridge known as Buzzard's Roost. Sherman sent Thomas' army to test the Confederate position then sent McPherson's army south to outflank the defenders. McPherson's forces were met by strong Confederate resistance and were forced to withdraw to await reinforcements. On 13 and 14 May Sherman maneuvered his armies towards Resaca, then sent General Hooker's XX Corps to attack the Confederate defenses there. Throughout the night and well into the next morning Hooker repeatedly attacked General Leonidas Polk's units, taking heavy casualties with each assault. As the Confederate lines began to waver under the intense Union attacks, Johnston implemented a tactical withdrawal of his and Polk's Army of Mississippi, reestablishing a defensive line near Cassville. Johnston had intended to launch a surprise attack from that position, but when the location was prematurely betrayed by General JB Hood, Johnston withdrew to Allatoona.

Sherman was gaining respect for his opponent. Rather than strike directly at the main Confederate position Sherman again attempted a flanking maneuver. Johnston had prepared for such a contingency by sending General Hook's corps to prepare defenses around New Hope Church. On 25 May Union troops, with Hooker's corps leading the flank assault, made three separate charges against the Confederate positions without success. The initial fighting was so fierce in the area dubbed 'Hell Hole' that both armies immediately shifted their main efforts to the New Hope Church area. On 28 May the fighting was resumed with increased intensity, but the Union forces could not gain an advantage. When Johnston's troops counterattacked the Union forces were thrown into chaos and forced to retreat. Sherman then decided to disengage and Johnston withdrew in turn to Kennesaw Mountain.

The weather changed during the first three weeks of June making further confrontations virtually impossible. There was a brief skirmish at Pine Mountain of 14 June where General Polk was killed, but Sherman was not prepared for battle until 27 June. Opposing Johnston's position at Kennesaw Mountain, Sherman had assembled more than 140 cannon which bombarded the Confederate defenses as a prelude to the attack. Thomas' army was drawn up into two massive columns facing the Confederate center. McPherson's army threatened the Confederate right and Schofield lay before the Confederate left. As Thomas' close order troops advanced, the Confederate volleys took an enormous toll and the casualty rate broke the advance. McPherson then took up the attack and although initially successful his troops were thrown back by a Confederate counter-attack. Schofield's army executed a feint on the Confederate left which had greater success than either of the other two attacks, outflanking and capturing a segment of the Confederate line. Johnston then acknowledged that renewed Union assaults on the next day might succeed in turning his left flank and withdrew during the night of 8 July to an excellent defensive position on the Chattahoochee River. Rather than again attempt to confront Johnston directly, Sherman left part of his forces to hold Johnston's attention and then marched northeast to Roswell, fording the river and forcing Johnston to withdraw to Atlanta or be outflanked.

Johnston's strategy had been successful. For two months he had maneuvered into positions which had cost Sherman high casualties to assault, while keeping Confederate losses to a minimum. However when the Confederate army reached Atlanta, Davis decided that he wanted to be rid of the 'faint-hearted defeatist' commander of his army. Davis was still angry about having been forced to replace Bragg and, although he wanted to put Bragg back into command, such an overt display of political favoritism and interference would not have been tolerated. Instead he allowed Bragg to choose the new commander and General John B Hood replaced Johnston on 17 July. Johnston, who had done the best possible job given the circumstances, resigned and left Georgia. A more impetuous, aggressive commander, Hood had appreciated Johnston's strategy but had a tendency to take greater risks than were necessary. Sherman knew this and yet was delighted to learn of the replacement, confident that he could goad Hood into action as he had not been able to do with Johnston.

The strong defenses built around Atlanta precluded direct attack, so Sherman laid siege to the city and waited for Hood to react. Sherman sent McPherson and Schofield east to destroy the rail links and supply routes from Decatur to Atlanta. He sent Thomas across Peach Tree Creek, north of the city and in doing so permitted a large gap to develop between Thomas' army and McPherson and Schofield. Johnston had devised plans to exploit just such a situation and Hood decided to attack. On 20 July Hood sent troops against Thomas to divide Sherman's armies. Although the plan had been well conceived, Hood failed to make a well-coordinated attack and the sporadic assaults were successfully repulsed with high Confederate casualties.

The Confederate forces withdrew into Atlanta and the three Union armies moved closer to the city perimeter. As they did so Hood decided to attempt a flanking maneuver with General Hardee's Corps around the left of McPherson's army. Hood intended to launch a frontal assault on McPherson's forces to coincide with that flank attack using Major General BF Cheatham's Division. At 1200 hours on 22 July Hardee launched his attack. It caught McPherson's troops by surprise and as McPherson rushed to organize his troops he was shot and killed. Although Hardee possessed a distinct advantage Hood had failed to implement the frontal assault at the same time. Hardee's momentum was lost and his assault floundered before Cheatham attacked. After repulsing Hardee the Union army was able to direct its full force against Cheatham's attack and repulse it as well. By dusk the offensive had resulted in more than 8000 Union and Confederate casualties and Hood had accomplished nothing.

From 23–28 July Sherman used his cavalry in an attempt to tighten the siege around Atlanta, but the effort was poorly managed and the forces nearly destroyed. On 28 July Hood again attempted to take the offensive without success and with high casualties. After further failures to encircle the city Sherman decided to adopt a more aggressive tactic. On 9 August he began a devastating, indiscriminate artillery bombardment of the city. Horrified by the unprecedented hostilities against a large civilian population, the mayor of Atlanta sent a message requesting that Sherman halt his 'barbaric actions.' Sherman's refusal had the effect of strengthening the will of the civilians and military within Atlanta to resist.

After several days of bombardment, Hood sent Major General Joseph Wheeler's cavalry on a wide sweep to Sherman's rear to create a diversion and draw Sherman's attention away from Atlanta. Although Wheeler harassed the Union army, Sherman continued his barrage, frustrated by the fact that the city had not surrendered. Two weeks after the artillery assault began Sherman again altered his tactics. He moved the main body of his army to the less fortified southern perimeter of the city. On 26 August Atlanta was quiet. Hood sent infantry units to investigate and they found Sherman's positions deserted. For several days the inhabitants of Atlanta celebrated what they believed was a Union retreat from the area. On the morning of 30 August their elation was shattered when Sherman's armies revealed themselves. Hood launched an immediate attack by Hardee's corps and although they fought valiantly for two days the Union superiority was too great. By nightfall on 31 August Hardee's 24,000-man corps had been reduced to 5000 able-bodied troops. The following morning Hood began to evacuate what remained of his army.

Although Sherman attempted to crush the retreating forces, Hardee's men fought an exceptional rearguard action which permitted Hood to escape. During the night of 1 September Hardee disengaged his forces and withdrew. The following day Atlanta surrendered. Sherman was now well on his way to accomplishing his objective.

After leaving Atlanta, Hood recaptured Allatoona and Dalton in October and continued on into Alabama. Although for several weeks Sherman sent troops to counter Hood's attempts to sever Union supply lines, he could not effectively engage the Confederate army and hold Atlanta at the same time. In November Sherman decided to send Thomas' army, with two corps as extra support, to pursue Hood. The remainder of Sherman's forces set out for Savannah, Georgia. To ensure that Confederate forces could not simply return to Atlanta Sherman destroyed the factories and burned the city. On 15 November he began his March to the Sea. The 60,000 Union soldiers under Sherman's command cut a path of destruction six-miles wide across Georgia. Sherman is credited with coining the phrase 'War is Hell' and he brought the full significance of that statement to the Southern people. On 21 December he marched into Savannah, fulfilling his promise to capture the city by Christmas.

Although the Southern people demanded that Hood return to Georgia to stop Sherman's march, Hood continued his campaign in Tennessee, convinced that by threatening Nashville he could force Sherman to leave Georgia. As Hood approached Nashville General Schofield's forces were unsuccessfully attempting to forestall Hood's advance until Thomas' army could arrive. Schofield was having great difficulty maneuvering his corps, but Hood made a serious tactical error which offset that advantage when he reached Spring Hill. After several engagements with Union forces Hood permitted his army to bivouac on 29 November, believing that he could deal with Schofield the following day. However during the night Schofield's forces moved into Franklin, Tennessee, entrenching themselves around the city.

When Hood realized what had occurred he was furious, blaming all his officers for the blunder. In a fit of temper he set his army in motion and threw his troops at the Union defenses as they arrived on the field. On that day no less than 13 different attacks were made on the Union positions and although at one point an assault appeared to be succeeding it was repulsed by Union reinforcements. When Hood finally halted the attacks, 6000 of his 40,000 troops were lost, five of his generals were dead including Patrick Cleburne, who had been an important figure in the Army of Tennessee and seven generals captured. Yet Hood would not give up his attempts to capture Nashville. Thomas held the city and, after Hood sent Forrest's cavalry to harass the Union forces, he decided to besiege Nashville. It was obvious that Hood had neither the men nor the means to conduct a siege and Thomas was willing to simply wait him out. However after two weeks Thomas received orders from General Grant to take the offensive. On 15 December Thomas attacked Hood's positions with a two to one superiority and in a well executed attack drove Hood from the field. Rather than concede defeat Hood withdrew to a second line

of defense to continue the battle. On 16 December Thomas' victory was even more decisive and Hood's army was forced to retreat across the Tennessee River, closely pursued by Union Troops.

By the last week of December 1864 the West was securely under Union control, Sherman was in Savannah and Grant was conducting his siege of Richmond and Petersburg. It was obvious that the war could not continue much longer. The year 1865 brought with it a sense of desperation within the Confederacy. Southerners, though dedicated to the cause they had been fighting for, were generally disheartened and pessimistic. The Union campaigns in the West had been completely successful. Sherman's Atlanta campaign and subsequent destructive path across Georgia had a serious impact on the South's ability to continue the war. Grant's campaign in the East and his continuing siege of Petersburg made the fall of the Confederate capital an imminent possibility. These actions are indicative of the success of Grant's 'total war' strategy and contributed to the war of attrition and to the destruction of the Southern people's will and ability to continue the war.

It was obvious that the South could no longer

Below: before evacuating Richmond the Confederates set fire to its military stores.

Left: the ruins of Richmond at the end of the Civil War.

anticipate England or France becoming directly involved in the war on behalf of the Confederacy. The Union blockade had reduced shipments of supplies from Europe to a mere fraction of their previous quantity and manpower availability had reached a critical level. Perhaps most importantly it at last became obvious to the Confederate government that it had interfered over much in the strategies of the war. On 6 February, with the overwhelming approval of the Confederate Congress, Jefferson Davis appointed Robert E Lee General-in-Chief of all Confederate armies. It was of course too little too late, and no doubt the Confederate government was attempting to absolve itself from further blame for the state of affairs in the army, but Lee was satisfied at last to be able to direct the Confederate war effort. He realized that the war was essentially over, but with his new powers Lee chose commanders and initiated strategies which he hoped would reduce the number of losses and lead the Confederate armies to a position from which they could negotiate an honorable peace settlement.

There was no lull in activity in the early winter months of 1865. Shortly after Lee's appointment

Sherman left Savannah to begin a new campaign into the Carolinas. His first objective was Columbia, capital of South Carolina. Sherman chose to bypass Charleston as it was already virtually destroyed and would be isolated once Columbia fell. Sherman decided to move his army by the most direct route to Columbia, through the 'impassable' swamps south of the city. On 17 February the Confederate militia in the city was taken completely by surprise when Sherman's army emerged from the swamps. The Confederate troops fled immediately, setting the storehouses in the city ablaze. In the panic and confusion the fires became uncontrollable and more than half of Columbia was destroyed. The Union army then continued its march and by the end of February Sherman had reached the North Carolina border.

From that point on there was a rapid succession of events. There were three main Union armies in eastern North Carolina. Sherman's army was moving toward Fayetteville from the south on a course for Goldsboro. The Fort Fisher garrison had captured nearby Wilmington, North Carolina, and were proceeding due north to rendezvous with Sherman. A third Union force was marching inland from the coast toward Kingston, which was less than 25 miles east of Goldsboro. There was virtually nothing that could save the state, but Lee hoped to forestall Sherman's arrival in the Petersburg area by delaying him near Goldsboro. Lee sent a personal plea to his friend Joseph E Johnston, who had retired from the army after Jefferson Davis removed him from command in Georgia, requesting that Johnston again assume command of the Army of Tennessee in North Carolina. Johnston accepted and in early March he took command of the army, which had been supplemented by militia and regular troops from the Carolinas.

Johnston decided to strike first at the Union forces which were approaching Kingston from the east. On 8 March he engaged these troops in the Battle of Kingston and finally defeated them after three days of battle, forcing the Union troops to retreat from the area. By 11 March Sherman had taken Fayetteville and was preparing to continue on his course. On 16 March part of Johnston's army, commanded by General Hardee, engaged Union forces at Averysboro but were quickly defeated. On 19 March the final battle in North Carolina was fought when Johnston attacked Sherman's forces at Bentonville. Although the initial stages of the battle produced a Confederate advantage, as additional Union forces arrived Johnston was forced onto the defensive. After holding for more than 48 hours Johnston had no alternative but to retreat, clearing the way for Sherman to march into Goldsboro and join up with the Fort Fisher troops.

As North Carolina fell the situation in Petersburg reached a critical state. Lee used his newly acquired command powers to initiate a strategy which would permit the Army of Northern Virginia to escape from the siege and rendezvous with Johnston. On 25 March 1865 a unit of Confederate engineers pretending to be deserters overpowered their 'captors' and occupied the Union line fortification Fort Stedman. Major General John B Gordon then led an attack with almost 33 percent of Lee's total army against the Union fortifications Fort Haskell and Fort McGilvery. Although the Confederate assault was initially successful Union reinforcements to the area overpowered Gordon's troops. At the opposite end of the lines around Petersburg, Lee began to move his army west toward Appomattox. Bad weather struck and hampered the maneuverability of the armies but did not deter Grant's pursuit of Lee. That pursuit was spearheaded by Generals Warren, AA Humphreys, and Sheridan.

Six days after the attack on Fort Stedman Confederate forces attacked Warren's V Corps near the Claiborne and White Oak crossroads but were repulsed. On 1 April Sheridan and Warren combined to attack the Confederates commanded by General Pickett on the White Oak Road in the Battle of Five Forks. Pickett's position was lost and his division virtually destroyed. On 2 April Grant ordered the Petersburg defenses taken and, although pockets of Confederate defenders resisted with great determination, within a few hours their positions were captured. During the defense General AP Hill was killed.

On 3 April Grant ordered a concerted attack on Richmond and Petersburg and while Lee's army fought rearguard actions the Confederate government fled the capital. By nightfall the Army of

Below: Lee and his staff ride away from Appomattox Court House after surrendering the Army of Northern Virginia.
Right: Union troops pose before Appomattox Court House.

48

Northern Virginia was in retreat toward Amelia Court House, having set fire to the military stores and factories before leaving the city. Richmond officially surrendered at approximately 2015 hours on 3 April.

Although Lee had only 30,000 troops remaining, he intended to make every attempt to rendezvous with Johnston. As various Confederate forces in Virginia maneuvered toward Amelia Court House, Grant sent his army on a route south of the main Confederate movement. Finally on 5 April Lee attempted to march south from Amelia Court House and found a strong Union position blocking his path. Rather than initiate a battle Lee began to move west once again toward Lynchburg. The Army of Northern Virginia was exhausted and hungry and its morale was deteriorating as it marched west throughout the night. On 6 April Union forces commanded by General Humphreys and General Charles Griffin, who had replaced Warren, attacked General Gordon's forces and Anderson's and Ewell's corps at different points on Sailor's Creek, capturing a large percentage of the Confederate supply wagons and taking some 8000 prisoners.

On 7 April Lee crossed to the northern bank of the Appomattox River and although he ordered the bridges to be burned after crossing several were not destroyed and the Union troops continued to harass Lee's rear. On 8 April supply trains destined for Lee's army were captured at Appomattox Station by Sheridan's cavalry which then positioned itself to block Lee's path once again. In the morning hours of 9 April Lee sent forces to break Sheridan's lines and although the Confederate forces appeared to be succeeding, two Union infantry corps commanded by General EOC Ord arrived to support the cavalry. The Union corps which had pursued Lee across Sailor's Creek and the Appomattox River then closed on Lee's rear. Lee's army was hopelessly trapped and the mental and physical condition of his troops so deteriorated that further attempts to escape would have been futile.

At 1600 hours on Palm Sunday 9 April 1865 Lee surrendered at Appomattox Court House. The meeting between the two generals in chief was solemn and cordial. One of Grant's first actions after the surrender was to send several days rations to the Confederate army. Five days later General Johnston surrendered to Sherman in Raleigh, North Carolina. Although fighting would continue in the West for several weeks, culminating in General Kirby Smith's surrender on 26 May to General Edward Canby, the American Civil War effectively ended with Lee's surrender.

5 THE WAR AT SEA

The influence of naval warfare on the events of the American Civil War was limited. At the outset of war the United States Navy consisted of approximately 90 vessels. Twenty-five seaworthy vessels had been sent on 'fool's errands' around the globe by the Secretary of the Navy John B Floyd. Floyd, a Confederate sympathizer, had sought to cripple the Union Navy's military potential for as long as possible. The remaining ships were moored at various ports awaiting repairs or refurbishment, with the 25-gun USS *Brooklyn* the only vessel of any consequence available for duty. Naval manpower was listed at approximately 9000 officers and men and, although the vast majority remained loyal to the Union, they were simply too few to undertake the task before them. It is little wonder that President Lincoln's institution of a naval blockade of Confederate ports was greeted with scorn by the Southern people. In conjunction with the blockade orders the Navy was also given responsibility for transporting troops and supplies and for conducting offensive operations against Confederate ports and fortifications.

The Federal Government bought or chartered all available vessels to fill the urgent demand for Union ships after the outbreak of war and ordered the building of eight new ships and 23 gunboats. Newly-appointed Secretary of the Navy Gideon Welles aggressively pursued the revitalization programs.

Below left: Captain Raphael Semmes commanded the Confederate commerce raider *Alabama*, which accounted for over 70 merchantmen.

Above: the officers of USS *Kearsarge* photographed after the successful action with the *Alabama*.

The civilian ships used on the high seas as blockade vessels were typically wooden sloops. Driven by both sails and steam engines, such vessels were usually equipped with twenty-two 9 inch cannon, port and starboard, and two 30 pound rifled cannon at the bow and stern. On inland waterways vessels with shallow draft were essential. The steam driven, paddle-wheel types were the most logical choice, as they had long been the primary river vessels. Armor plating was occasionally added to such vessels, their main targets being enemy river fortifications. Although their armament varied, generally such gunboats mounted eight to twelve cannon in sizes ranging from 9 inch smooth-bore cannon to 12 pound 'Napoleons' and 24 pound howitzers.

Although the Union Navy was in a deplorable state when hostilities began, the Confederacy had no navy whatsoever. They naturally turned to their trading partners in Europe, primarily Britain and France, for the development of a naval force. The South did not possess the facilities for large-scale ship construction, nor the expertise, and new vessels were commissioned in England by the Confederate government. Other vessels and their crews were hired by the Confederacy to act as privateers and blockade runners to ensure that the flow of goods and materiels between

Europe and the Confederacy was maintained. The CSS *Sumter* and particularly the CSS *Alabama*, both commanded by Captain Raphael Semmes, were two of the most noted and successful of the Confederate privateers. Their reign on the high seas lasted from June 1861 until June 1864 and in that time the *Alabama* alone plundered and sank more than 71 Union vessels.

As the Union and Confederacy struggled to bring their naval forces onto a war footing a new class of vessel was developing – the ironclad. The concept of wooden ships modified as armor plated vessels had been tested during the Crimean War, but the American Civil War introduced the first ships built specifically as ironclad vessels. In the South the concept was developed as a defensive measure to protect ports and fortifications accessible by water. The first Confederate ironclad was built through the modification of the scuttled Union ship *Merrimack*. In July 1861 work began and when completed the vessel was rechristened CSS *Virginia*. It was armed with three 8 inch cannon, two 6 inch cannon and two 7 inch swivel guns and a forward ram. An unwieldy, cumbersome ship, its maneuverability problems were not considered to be of major concern as the vessel was intended primarily for a defensive role. Commanded by Captain Franklin Buchanan, former Superintendent of the Annapolis Naval Academy and Commander of the Washington Navy Yard, the *Virginia* made her maiden voyage with 350 crew members on 8 March 1862.

After leaving Norfolk, Virginia, she sailed to Chesapeake Bay where five Union vessels commanded by Admiral Goldsborough lay. The USS *Minnesota*, USS *Congress* and the USS *Roanoke* were fifty gun vessels of the same class as the original *Merrimack*. The fifty-two gun USS *Saint Lawrence* and the twenty-four gun USS *Cumberland* completed the small fleet. The officers and men of the Union vessels were taken by surprise when the *Virginia* approached to within 1500 yards of the *Congress* and opened fire. The *Congress'* crew rallied and returned the fire, but were amazed when their shells ricocheted off the hull of the Confederate vessel. The *Congress* was seriously damaged and the *Virginia* maneuvered to attack the *Cumberland*. Within the hour the *Cumberland* sank in the shallow waters of the bay. The attention of the *Virginia* then reverted to the *Congress*, whose captain had beached the ship rather than let it sink. After a punishing barrage the *Congress* struck her colors, indicating surrender. But as Buchanan moved in to claim his prize artillery fired on the *Virginia* from the shores. In reply Buchanan set the *Congress* ablaze, but was himself wounded in the exchange. Lieutenant Jones took command. Darkness was approaching and the remaining three Union vessels had run aground while attempting to maneuver to protect the *Congress* and the *Cumberland*. Jones decided to withdraw and resume the assault in daylight.

On that same day a Union ironclad, the *Monitor* was approaching Chesapeake Bay. Designed by John Ericsson, it was the first American vessel built specifically as an iron ship. Resembling a flat barge with a pill-box at its center, the *Monitor* was equipped with two Dahlgreen 11 inch cannon mounted in the revolving central turret. The *Monitor*'s low profile made it extremely unstable on the open sea and on that maiden voyage her captain, Lieutenant Commander John L Worden, was tempted to abandon the vessel on at least two occasions. The *Monitor* finally arrived in the bay on the night of 8 March, while the *Congress* still burned and Worden was informed of the presence of a Confederate ironclad.

At 0630 hours on 9 March the *Virginia* re-appeared, on a course for the stranded *Minnesota*. As it approached, *Virginia* passed near the *Monitor*, which Jones mistook for a harbor buoy. When the *Monitor* opened fire Jones quickly realized that the maneuverability and speed of the Union vessel made it far superior to his own. After an ineffective exchange of fire between the ironclads, Jones attempted to ram the *Monitor*. That attempt damaged the bow of the *Virginia*, but not the one inch armor plated hull of the *Monitor*. Jones then turned from the Union ironclad to engage the *Minnesota*, while the *Monitor* maneuvered to protect the wooden ship. While maneuvering the *Virginia* ran aground and became easy prey for the *Monitor*. But a volley from the Confederate vessel struck the *Monitor*, dazing Captain Worden. With the

captain unable to give orders to the contrary the helmsman of the Union ironclad steamed on his previous course, carrying the *Monitor* away from the *Virginia*. Before the *Monitor* could reverse course the crew of the *Virginia* freed their vessel and steamed to the opposite side of the bay.

The Battle of Hampton Roads between the ironclads ended in stalemate, but three Union wooden ships were destroyed. The confrontation demonstrated the obvious superiority of ironclad vessels over wooden ships and the advantages of the Union ironclad design. The South would continue to alter vessels as it had done the *Merrimack* to defend Southern ports, while the North created new, more seaworthy ironclad designs with added firepower, geared for an offensive role. The combination of ironclads and wooden ships was employed by the Union, resulting in overwhelming superiority on the sea.

After a high degree of Union success along the Southern coast and on inland waterways, which included the capture of New Orleans and Vicksburg, a naval battle of major significance was fought in Mobile Bay in 1864. Mobile, Alabama, was one of the last remaining ports of major import in the Confederacy. Admiral David Farragut, Commander of the Western Gulf Blockading Squadron, had long sought permission to capture Mobile. The strength of the fortifications around the city had steadily increased and the harbor housed a small squadron of

Confederate vessels, including the *Tennessee*, the most heavily armed and armored Confederate ironclad. The *Tennessee* was a renovated vessel, with the hull covered with three layers of two inch iron plate. Its armament included four 6.4 inch Brooke rifled cannon for broadside volleys and two 7 inch Brooke rifled guns on pivot mountings fore and aft. The bow of the vessel was also equipped with a powerful ram. However the *Tennessee* also possessed all the least desirable traits of Confederate ironclads. The maximum speed of the vessel was under six knots and her heavy armor and armament made the vessel extremely cumbersome in the water. The gun ports were covered by shutters, which if damaged would prohibit the firing of the cannon. Perhaps the worst feature of the craft was the fact that the main drive chain was exposed across the deck. Although covered by an iron plate, damage to the chain would immobilize the vessel.

Franklin Buchanan, commander of the *Virginia*, had been promoted to admiral and given command of the Mobile Squadron. In cooperation with the land defenses of Brigadier General Gabriel Rains, Buchanan mined Mobile Bay, leaving a narrow channel through which vessels could pass. By early August 1864 Farragut had received permission to carry out an attack on Mobile. His squadron had been complemented by the addition of four ironclads: the

Above: the Confederate ironclad *Virginia* (left) in action with the *Monitor* during the Battle of Hampton Roads. Right: the crew of the *Monitor* pictured in July 1862.

single turret *Manhattan* and *Tecumseh* and the double turret *Chickasaw* and *Winnebago*. Union land forces, under the command of Major General Gordon Granger, had also arrived to assist in the attack. Before the battle Farragut and an aide, Lieutenant Commander JC Watson, staged mock battles with miniature vessels to develop an effective strategy. Finally it was decided that the fleet would be divided into two columns. The ironclads would proceed first through the channel single-file. The remaining wooden ships would be grappled in pairs of one small gunboat and one larger vessel. Once within the inner bay the ships would separate, sending the ironclads and larger vessels primarily against the *Tennessee*, while the gunboats engaged the non-ironclad ships.

At dawn on 5 August Farragut launched his attack. By 0700 hours the fleet was engaged in an artillery duel with the harbor fortification, Fort Morgan. During the exchange the *Tennessee*, followed by several smaller gunboats moved into the channel. Caught between the mined waters and the artillery fire from Fort Morgan, Farragut ordered the *Brooklyn* forward to lead the column of ships through the channel. In apparent confusion the *Brooklyn* swung about, blocking the channel and heading for the minefields. The *Tecumseh*, which led the ironclad column, then broke formation and steamed directly toward the *Tennessee* through the mines. Within minutes she had struck a mine and sunk with her captain and 90 crew members on board.

Farragut's well organized plans were in chaos. The *Brooklyn* and Farragut's flagship the *Hartford* were being subjected to an intense artillery barrage. Rather than allow his fleet to be destroyed piecemeal by the fortress batteries, Farragut signalled that he intended to pursue his original tactics. The only path to the inner bay lay through the mined waters and as other vessels frantically signalled the danger, Farragut made his famous reply, 'Damn the torpedos! Full steam ahead!' He set the *Hartford* on a course through the minefield, followed by the remainder of his fleet. Although mine primers could be heard activating, not one ship was damaged and the inner bay was reached. With renewed confidence the Union vessels emerged and Buchanan set the *Tennessee* directly at the *Hartford* to ram it. The Union flagship managed to alter course and avoid the ram, delivering a full broadside barrage. The cannon failed to damage the *Tennessee* but forced the *Gaines* and *Morgan*, escort gunboats for the Confederate ironclad, to withdraw. The third Confederate gunboat, the *Selma* maneuvered to the bow of the *Hartford* and fired into the ship. In response Farragut released the lines which had bound his vessel to the smaller *Metacomet* that it might engage the *Selma*. The *Tennessee* attempted several more unsuccessful maneuvers to ram Union vessels then retreated toward the protection of harbor artillery.

Above and right: two views of the Battle of Mobile Bay. Below: the Confederate submersible *CL Hunley*.

The battle was temporarily quiet and Farragut considered his next move, aware that his three remaining ironclads would have to be relied upon to deal with the *Tennessee*. Buchanan then turned his vessel to continue the engagement. In the confines of the inner bay the Union ships maneuvered to catch and ram the Confederate ironclad. The *Monogahela* and the *Lackawanna* were the first to make contact, damaging their own hulls but inflicting no damage on the ironclad. The *Hartford* then unsuccessfully attempted to ram the *Tennessee* and both vessels fired into one another at close range. The *Hartford*'s hull was damaged further when its maneuvers resulted in a collision with the *Lackawanna*. Frustrated by the fleet's inability to damage the Confederate ironclad, Farragut ordered the wooden ships to stand off while the monitors attacked. The *Chickasaw* was the first to approach the *Tennessee*,

As the concept of iron ships was being explored another naval concept was being developed. The idea for a 'submersible torpedo boat' or submarine had been considered since before the American Revolution. The Union made several attempts to develop such a vessel and succeeded in producing the Intelligent Whale. It was an extremely unstable vessel and never saw combat. The South was particularly intrigued with the concept and its possibilities for use against the Union's blockade. Several variations of the main design were unsuccessfully attempted. Finally the David, was constructed, named for the Biblical king in reference to the small submersible's role as a giant-ship killer. The expulsion of steam from the propulsion system meant that the ship had to remain partially above water, making it suitable primarily for night attacks. The armament of submersibles was a spar torpedo, an explosive device attached to a long pole mounted on the bow of the submersible which detonated on impact with the enemy vessel. The adverse effects of that torpedo on the submersible were only some of the many flaws. During the maiden voyage of the first David the vessel sank when it was swamped by the wake of a passing vessel. Recovered in October 1863 that same David attacked the USS *Ironsides* near Charleston Harbor. The submersible failed to damage the Union ironclad and was again swamped and sunk.

Further Confederate attempts were made to modify the design of the submersible. In 1863 Horace L Hunley developed a craft which was powered by eight crewmen who sat and turned a crank which operated the propeller. During a test of the vessel in October 1863 it sank, drowning the crew and inventor. Refloated and christened the CSS *HL Hunley* the vessel was captained by Lieutenant George E Dixon and manned with an all volunteer infantry crew. On 17 February the *Hunley* attacked and sank the USS *Housatonic* and, although achieving the distinction of being the first submersible to sink its target, the *Hunley* went down with the Union vessel.

The use of naval forces during the Civil War was merely a sideshow compared to the land war being waged. Despite the battles fought and lives lost, as well as the innovations and advances in naval warfare, the primary function of the Union Navy was the successful blockade and elimination of Southern ports. Conversely the principal role of the naval vessels employed by the Confederacy was the disruption of Union merchant and blockade traffic and the defense of major ports and fortifications. As the funds of the Confederate government dwindled so did their available navy. After 1863 the blockade became a virtual wall around the Confederate coastline and an integral part of the war of attrition being waged by the Union. One thing however was made abundantly clear; the art of naval warfare had entered a new era.

delivering a devastating barrage which began to dislodge the armor plates of the Confederate vessel. Other Union vessels joined the attack and it was not long before the vital drive chain had been destroyed. The *Tennessee*'s smokestack was gone and the gunport shutters were jammed. Finally the *Manhattan* raked the Confederate ironclad sealing its fate.

Five hours after the start of the battle Buchanan surrendered aboard the *Tennessee*. The fortifications of Mobile Bay fell shortly thereafter, but the city itself was never captured. Farragut had however achieved his goal and the contributions of Mobile to the war effort were eliminated. Union casualties during the naval engagement were 145 killed and 174 wounded. The sinking of the *Tecumseh* was notorious as the worst naval combat disaster until World War II. Buchanan's losses were listed at 12 killed, 20 wounded and some 300 captured.

6 ARMS AND ARMIES

Much like the Navy, at the outbreak of war the United States Army was ill equipped and undermanned. The Regular Army consisted of no more than 13,000 officers and men, a figure regulated by legislation of the Federal Government. The isolationist policies and distrust of a large standing army had dictated that the numbers of military personnel be kept at a minimum. In the event of national emergency it was the citizen soldiers, the militia, who would be called upon to augment the Regular Army. The inadequacies and ineffectiveness of that militia would soon be discovered when armed conflict between the North and South began.

On 15 April 1861 after the fall of Fort Sumter, Lincoln issued orders for the induction of 75,000 militiamen into active duty. The implementation of such an order within the Army was quite as impossible as was the original blockade orders for the Navy. Through inactivity the militia system had virtually ceased to function. And, as the troops inducted were required to serve for only three months in a given year, there was not time to recruit, train and employ such troops in the war effort. That service ruling was rapidly changed in both the North and South, extending periods of enlistment to between one and three years.

As tens of thousands were inducted into the army, it was quickly discovered that men were being brought into the service who were either physically or mentally unsuited for active duty. By 1863 rigid standards had been laid down stating the requirements and guidelines which must be followed. Those requirements included tests to detect mental illness or retardation, age and stature, general physical conditions and explicit physical illnesses or disabilities which would bar the prospective recruit from enlistment. Those basic qualification standards were the foundation of the system used in the present day. Throughout the course of the Civil War hundreds of thousands of white males would pass through that system. Additionally some 500,000 immigrants, 3500 American Indians and 186,000 Blacks fought for the Union and Confederacy.

Once induction was accomplished, training became the next major stumbling block. Inadequate training facilities, a shortage of experienced instructors, and a general confusion about the most effective training procedures all contributed to the lack of preparedness within the early field armies. The results were poor discipline and morale and the inability of the average soldier to react on the battlefield. The fundamental difference between the Union and Confederate armies in the initial stages of the war was the skill and expertise of the Confederate officer corps, most of whom had resigned their United States Army commissions to answer the call of their seceded states.

Equipping the troops posed yet another problem. Uniforms were naturally one of the first items required by the new recruits. Initially the demand for uniforms far exceeded the supplies and troops appeared on the field dressed in a wide variety of military and civilian dress. The United States Army had a regulation dark blue uniform, which was soon adopted by the Union as standard dress. The Confederates devised their uniform in the same style but chose the readily available 'cadet gray' cloth. Along with the uniform certain items were standard equipment for the average infantry soldier. The knapsack was originally used to carry the soldier's personal possessions and change of clothing, but it soon gave way to the more practical blanket roll. The soldier's personal belongings were rolled inside his woollen blanket, which was then tied off and slung over his shoulder. Another item which appeared later in the war was the haversack, which was primarily used to carry food and cooking supplies. Canteens, knives, and ammunition belts were only a few of the possible additions to the troop's personal equipment.

The most important article issued to the troops was their weapon. At the beginning of the war several different muskets and rifled muskets were employed. For the Union the United States Rifle Musket 1855 and the United States Rifle Musket 1861 were most widely used, replacing the unreliable United States Rifle Musket 1841, 'Mississippi Rifle.' The Model 1855 had a volley range of up to 500 yards with an accurate individual range of 150 yards, with the most popular variation being the 'Harper's Ferry Rifle.' Approximately 47,000 to 50,000 of the Model 1855 were produced between 1857 and 1861. The Model 1861 was produced at the Springfield Armory, Massachusetts, and became known as the 'Spring-

field Musket.' It improved on the 1855 design, altering the primer system and making the weapon volley effective to 1000 yards and accurate for individual fire to 300 yards. Its rapid rate of fire capability of five or six rounds per minute made the Springfield extremely popular. Approximately 900,000 were produced for use during the Civil War.

For the Confederacy the primary weapon before 1863 was the United States Percussion Musket, Model 1842, though a larger percentage of Confederate troops than Union soldiers used personal firearms brought with them to the army. The Model

Far left: a non-commissioned officer of the Engineers, Union Army, poses for a studio portrait.
Left: an infantryman of the Confederate Army in the distinctive 'cadet grey' uniform.
Below: color bearers of the 7th Illinois Infantry.

Above: blacks enlisted in the Union army and fought bravely in a number of engagements, notably the Battle of Petersburg

Right: the Parrot Rifle was one of the first rifled field guns to be used by the United States Army.
Below right: the hand grenade proved to be especially useful in the siege operations of the Civil War. However they were unreliable weapons, which were prone to explode prematurely.

1842 was a smoothbore, muzzle-loading weapon, which although reliable had a rate of fire of only two or three rounds per minute and an effective range of only 100 yards. That limited range and fire rate gave an obvious advantage to Union troops. To compensate for the inability of the South to produce an effective rifle musket, weapons were purchased abroad, primarily from Britain. The British Enfield became the most popular. The Enfield had an accurate range of 1100 yards when fired in volleys and an individual range of 500 yards. In that respect it was superior to the Springfield, but its rate of fire was no better than that of the Model 1842. The exact number of Enfield rifle muskets purchased is not confirmed, but estimates range from 200,000 to 800,000.

The favored weapon of the cavalry was the carbine, which was best suited to the mounted troops' particular needs. The Sharps Carbine was a single shot, lever operated, breech loading weapon with an effective range of 400 yards. The Spencer Carbine was a repeater rifle, which held eight rounds and could deliver twenty-one rounds per minute. The Henry Rifle, which appeared late in the war and was the predecessor of the Winchester Rifle, was a .44 caliber weapon which could fire fifteen rounds in approx-

imately eleven seconds. Some 100,000 Sharps, 200,000 Spencer and 10,000 Henry rifles were used during the war. In effect, the American Civil War served as a proving ground for experimentation with the rifle musket. Muzzle loading, which involved several defined steps for reloading, kept the rate of fire at a minimum and increased the opportunity for error. Thus ideas were formulated for a breech loaded, magazine-cartridge weapon. The Sharps was one such design. However, the Sharps was a single action carbine and the concept of a rapid fire weapon drew increased attention. Experimentation gave rise to the Spencer Rifle and the Henry, which in one simple motion ejected the spent casing, fed a new round into the chamber and cocked the weapon.

However further development continued. In July 1856 a patent had been awarded to CE Barnes for a crank-operated, rapid-fire weapon. The idea was given little credibility until 1861 when the Union Repeating Gun or Ager Gun was developed. The weapon closely resembled a coffee grinder of that era, using a crank and hopper ammunition feeding mechanism for fire. Although the Union Repeating Gun could fire 120 rounds per minute to a range of 1000 yards, it was unreliable with a tendency to over-

records were not kept, but from 150,000 to 500,000 Colts were used during the Civil War. The Remington, approximately 120,000 of which were used, was also a single-action, six round weapon, available in .44 and .35 caliber. The .44 caliber Starr revolver was later developed and was the first to effectively employ a self-cocking mechanism. It could fire a cartridge or be loaded with powder and ball. However it was the least popular of the revolvers and by contrast only 40,000 were actually used. Other weapons included the saber, sword, and bayonet. The cavalry lance and the antiquated pike were also considered, particularly by the Confederacy. Their impractical role on a battlefield which was being dominated by rifle fire was soon realized.

Trained, armed and equipped, the troops were organized into fighting units. United States Regular Army regiments were few, but they were organized with 100 men per company, eight companies per battalion, and two to four battalions per regiment. The volunteer Union army of the Civil War eliminated the battalion, incorporating ten companies of 100 men each into a regiment, though in actual fact the size of companies averaged sixty to eighty men. The regimental strengths therefore varied to between 800 and 1000 men. Both the Union and Confederate armies were then organized with brigades of four or five regiments each. The Union army combined three brigades to equal one division of approximately 6000 men. The Confederacy combined four to six brigades into a larger division classification of approximately 9000 men. Corps, which were the primary fighting

heat and misfire. The following year the Confederacy introduced the Williams Gun which was a single-barrel, breech-loading weapon which could fire 18 to 20 rounds per minute. However it suffered from all the inadequacies of the Union Repeating Gun and was similarly unpopular with the troops. It was not until Richard J Gatling, known as the father of the modern machine gun, developed the Model 1862 Gatling Gun that an effective design was achieved. The weapon used a system of rotating six gun barrels in front of a loading mechanism, firing each barrel in rapid succession as the operational crank was turned. Although Gatling tried for several years to introduce the Gatling Gun to the Union army, it was not until 1866 that full recognition was given to the potential of the weapon.

Another weapon popular with the cavalry and officers was the revolver. Although several American and European models appeared, the Colt and Remington were favored. The Colt pistol revolver had three basic variations during the Civil War; the Dragoon the Army and the Navy models. All Colt revolvers were single action weapons, which required the hammer to be cocked after each fire. Their effective range was between twenty and fifty yards. Accurate units of both the North and South, were composed of four divisions, but each Confederate corps had 50 percent more troops than its Union counterpart.

The cavalry was similarly organized, with 100 men forming a company, two or three companies forming a squadron, and four to six squadrons comprising a regiment. Although this was the rule it was widely acknowledged that the average Union cavalry regiment contained 250 to 350 men. Confederate cavalry regiments were divided into ten companies of 100 men each, but like the North their active strength was much lower at approximately 500 troopers per regiment. The primary difficulty encountered within the cavalry was the availability of adequate numbers of horses. Confederate cavalry was fundamentally different from Union cavalry in that the majority of Southern regiments were organized and funded by private citizens who were often also their commanding officers.

As the design of the rifle musket advanced, so too did the development of artillery. The basic cannon in the early war years was the 12 pound Napoleon Gun Howitzer. A smooth bore cannon it could fire four canister, or two aimed shots per minute with an effective maximum shot range of 2000 yards. There was also a 6 pound Napoleon Gun Howitzer which fired the same type round at approximately the same rate, but its effective range was 500 yards less than the 12 pound model. In 1863 the 3 inch Rodman or 3 inch Ordinance Rifle/Gun artillery piece was developed by the Union. It was a light weight, maneuverable rifled cannon and it was extremely effective as a close range weapon. Its effective long range was 2000 yards, but the Rodman was known to strike accurately at up to 4000 yards. It was a sought-after prize by the Confederate armies and attempts were always made to capture or salvage it from the battlefields. A variation of the 3.00 caliber Rodman was the Parrott which could deliver ten and twenty pound rounds.

Imported breech-loading rifled artillery pieces included the British 12 pound Blakely, 12 pound Whitworth and 12 pound Armstrong. These weapons, though extensively employed by the Confederacy in the initial stages of the war, were soon relegated to range detection service as they were prone to misfire and explosion. Various attempts were made, particularly in the South to develop new cannon models, some of which were extremely impractical, but almost all attempts met with failure.

Artillery, the 'Queen of the battlefield,' was divided into light and heavy classification; light for direct battlefield support and heavy for offensive and defensive fortification roles. The average Union artillery battery consisted of four to six cannon of the same caliber, with a six- or seven-man crew, limber, and horse team per cannon. Ammunition wagons, repair and maintenance equipment and spare horses and

Above: sutlers accompanying the Union army sold the troops canned food to supplement their rations.
Below: farriers and blacksmiths followed the armies.

Civil War rarely succeeded. Open order troop advance would become the accepted norm. Not only was fire potential increased by the weapons, but also by the tactics of the armies. Entrenchment, for offensive and defensive capabilities and protection, became a pronounced characteristic of Civil War infantry battlefield deployment. Thus a self-perpetrating cycle was begun. Increased firepower forced troops to create or utilize defensive positions. The massed firepower of entrenched troops forced offensive forces to employ skirmish-type assault tactics. The need for such a change in tactics was clearly illustrated in the carnage which resulted from Burnside's assaults at Fredericksburg and Pickett's Charge at Gettysburg.

Weapons and tactics changed and old ideas were given new meaning during the American Civil War. The railroad became an integral part of the maneuverability and sustenance of field armies. The concept of a rail car mounted with a heavy cannon for bombardment of fortifications was also first applied during the war. The telegraph became an effective method of rapid communication between armies and between commanders in the field and policymakers in the capitals. Hot air balloons, essentially recreational devices, were employed in the military for observation and to direct artillery fire. Professor Thaddeus Lowe commanded one such 'Balloon Corps' of seven craft and although greater potentials would later be discovered for the balloon, during the Civil War such potential was not fully recognized. One direct result of the use of balloon's ability to reconnoiter from the air was the development of camouflage techniques which had never been necessary before.

Yet another non-military invention which would later find its way to practical military application was the camera. Largely through the photographic efforts of one man, Mathew Bradey, the Civil War was fully documented in picture form. Such documentation of armies would later lead to the use of photography as an intelligence gathering source. Barbed wire fencing material also appeared on the battlefield. First used at Drewry's Bluff in 1864, barbed wire was strung in front of the Union defenses. The effects of the wire on advancing infantry are obvious and, although at the time it was considered a barbaric addition to the battlefield, it would become an integral part of the defensive structure of later wars. Missile or hand-thrown weapons were taken one step beyond their explosive capabilities when stink bombs were introduced. Primarily used against entrenched troops, their noxious gases were released on detonation, forcing the troops from their defenses. Such stink bombs were the forerunner of the deadly gases of World War I. Variations of old concepts and the development of more sophisticated weapons indicated that the American Civil War was indeed a transitional stage in the evolution of warfare.

limbers also accompanied each battery. The more mobile horse artillery batteries were composed of six to eight cannon with six or seven mounted crewmen and the same general accompaniment of regular artillery batteries. Artillery batteries were organized into battalions of two to five batteries each with two to four battalions per artillery brigade. Ideally each army corps had at least one artillery brigade. The organization and distribution of Confederate artillery was relatively the same with one major difference. The Confederate armies were forced, through the deficiencies of their artillery acquisitions, to combine cannon of different caliber within the same battery. This resulted in a great deal of difficulty maintaining adequate ammunition supplies and as the war progressed every effort was made to bring uniformity to the artillery batteries.

Other explosive, missile-type weapons included rockets and grenades, though the inconsistencies and dangers involved in their use made them extremely unpopular with the average troops. Various changes in the employment of strategies and tactics were also begun during the Civil War. Increased, more accurate fire potential demanded the abandonment of close order, massive attacks, which when applied during the

7 WITH MALICE TOWARD NONE

Below: Andersonville camp held some 32,000 Union prisoners.

The ending of armed conflict with the Union victorious proved that the initial differences between the capabilities of the North and South to wage war had been insurmountable for the weaker Confederacy.

Near the end of the war, with victory a certainty, Lincoln devised plans for the reunification of the States and the reconstruction of the war-torn South. His policy, 'With malice toward none and charity for all,' would be cast aside after his assassination on 14 April 1865. Long opposed to so forgiving an attitude, the Radical Republican Representatives in Washington had also acted early to preserve their control in Congress. In July 1864 the Wade-Davis Bill, which listed stringent regulations for the re-admittance of Confederate States to the Union was presented to Lincoln, who refused to sign it. The Bill, which served to frighten and alienate the Southern people, indicated the vengeful sentiment of the Radical Republicans.

After the assassination Andrew Johnson took the office of President and although initially harsh, he soon indicated that he intended to support Lincoln's proposals. In his various efforts to do so Johnson succeeded in antagonizing even the moderate Republicans, but for a brief period there was relative calm as attempts were made to reestablish order.

Cities had been devastated and the combined effects of the war and the loss of the slave labor force meant that adequate shelter and food supplies were a serious problem. As the South began to rebuild, it soon became evident that their efforts to conform to the policies dictated for reconstruction did not sufficiently satisfy the Radical Republicans. It was decided that the former Confederate states did not rank as states or even as territories but as 'conquered provinces.' If Johnson had been less rigid in his positions the Radical Republicans might have been willing to compromise. As it was they banded together and locked Southern Representatives out of Congress in December 1865, taking full control of the legislation of the Reconstruction process. The Fourteenth Amendment to the Constitution was passed establishing a Civil Rights code applicable to the freed slaves. With the exception of Tennessee the Confederate states refused to ratify the Amendment. From that point on the complete subjugation of the resistant Southern states was the goal of the Radicals. There was chaos in the South and in March 1867 the Republicans overrode Johnson's veto and passed the Reconstruction Act. The ten Southern states which had rejected the Fourteenth Amendment were divided into military districts with Federal Army regulars representing law and order. Former Confederate leaders were relieved of voting rights and the right to hold political office. Freed slaves were given those rights, which had to be guaranteed by the governments of each state.

A long and bitter dispute arose and as confrontations between North and South continued a deep-seated resentment and hostility was born. The South struck back against black freedmen when it could not strike at the perpetrators of Reconstruction. It was only once the intensity of a senseless revenge against the South abated that the nation could begin to progress as a whole. Unfortunately the Reconstruction Era divided the nation as the violence of the war had not, leaving scars which would never be completely healed and a legacy which would never be completely forgotten.

INDEX

The author would like to thank Adrian Hodgkins, the designer, Penny Murphy who compiled the index and Richard Natkiel who prepared the maps. The following agencies supplied the illustrations.

Bison Picture Library: p 12 (right)
Library of Congress: pp 1, 10, 13, 28, 29, 30, 32 (top), 49, 53, 58, 62–63
The Mansell Collection: pp 35, 38, 46–47, 52–53, 55
Map © Richard Natkiel 1981: p 31
Peter Newark's Western Americana: pp 2–3, 4–5, 7 (top), 8, 11, 12 (left), 15–23, 24 (right), 27, 37 (left), 39–43, 47, 48, 51, 54, 57, 58–59, 60–61
New York Historical Society: p 9
Robert Hunt Library: pp 24 (left), 25, 32 (bottom), 54–55, 59
Smithsonian Institution: pp 14, 37 (right)
US Navy: pp 7 (bottom), 50